# HAMLET OR HECUBA

# Hamlet or Hecuba:
## The Intrusion of the Time into the Play

### Carl Schmitt

Translated by David Pan and Jennifer R. Rust

Telos Press Publishing
New York

Printed in the United States of America
14 13 12 11 10 09  1 2 3 4 5

ISBN: 978-0-914386-42-1

Library of Congress Cataloging-in-Publication Data

Schmitt, Carl, 1888-1985.
  [Hamlet oder Hekuba. English]
  Hamlet or Hecuba : the intrusion of the time into the play / Carl Schmitt ; translated [from the German] by David Pan and Jennifer R. Rust.
    p. cm.
  ISBN-13: 978-0-914386-42-1 (pbk. : alk. paper)
  ISBN-10: 0-914386-42-5 (pbk. : alk. paper)
  1. Shakespeare, William, 1564-1616. Hamlet. 2. Hamlet (Legendary charac-
ter) 3. Benjamin, Walter, 1892-1940. 4. English drama (Tragedy)--History and
criticism--Theory, etc. 5. Tragedy--History and criticism--Theory, etc. I. Pan,
David, 1963- II. Rust, Jennifer R. III. Title.
  PR2807.S3613 2009
  822.3'3--dc22
            2009030514

Telos Press Publishing
431 East 12th Street
New York, NY 10009

www.telospress.com

# CONTENTS

PREFACE TO THE ENGLISH TRANSLATION      vii

TRANSLATORS' ACKNOWLEDGEMENTS      xiii

INTRODUCTION: SCHMITT AND SHAKESPEARE      xv

HAMLET OR HECUBA: THE INTRUSION OF THE
TIME INTO THE PLAY      1

  Preface      5

  Introduction      7

  The Taboo of the Queen      11

  The Figure of the Avenger      19

  The Source of the Tragic      32

  Results      50

  Appendix One: Hamlet as Heir to the Throne      53

  Appendix Two: On the Barbaric Character of
    Shakespearean Drama: A Response to Walter
    Benjamin's *The Origin of German Tragic Drama*      59

AFTERWORD: HISTORICAL EVENT AND MYTHIC
MEANING IN CARL SCHMITT'S *HAMLET OR HECUBA* 69

# PREFACE TO THE ENGLISH TRANSLATION

David Pan

This volume represents the culmination of a process dating back to 1986, a year when there was as yet very little interest in Carl Schmitt in the U.S. and when I had just graduated from college with a degree in English and German, looking for something to do with my newfound language skills. At the time, Paul Piccone, the founding editor of *Telos*, was motivated by Gary Ulmen to assemble a special issue of *Telos* devoted to Schmitt. Without denying Schmitt's Nazi past, Piccone and Ulmen recognized the importance of confronting some of his key themes, especially sovereignty and political theology, that had lost currency outside of his work. Contrary to much subsequent scholarship that sees Schmitt as concerned primarily with executive power, they argued in their introduction that Schmitt's theories investigate the link between politics and substantive values, without which "qualitative social change would be impossible." As *Telos* did not have the funds to pay for translations, it relied on students like me to get things done for the price of a byline. My undergraduate advisor, then-editorial associate and current editor Russell Berman suggested to Piccone that I translate "The Source of the Tragic" as well as "Appendix Two" from *Hamlet or Hecuba*, which appeared in the second of two *Telos* issues devoted to Schmitt in 1987.

This project would have fit well with *Telos*'s history of introducing modern European thought to an American audience if it had not been for the circumstance that Schmitt was a figure whose conservative tendencies and Nazi past made him into the equivalent of a "third rail" in American intellectual life. As it was, the general response was to shoot the messenger. Readers such as Stephen Holmes, Jürgen Habermas, and Richard Wolin (an editorial associate who resigned in the wake of the Schmitt issues) accused this historically left-leaning journal of promoting the most politically regressive and intellectually suspect material imaginable, in addition to attempting to rehabilitate the work of a documented anti-Semite and the "crown jurist" of the Third Reich. Though his personal history with the Nazis certainly cannot be overlooked and indeed may very well have been linked to the development of his ideas, the relationship between politics and values that his work raises are not just the province of the radical right. The journal's subsequent shift toward topics such as populism, tradition, federalism, and religion was not a right-wing break from the journal's roots in Western Marxism and critical theory but an attempt to think through competing alternatives to critical theory's own critique of liberalism.

Even though *Telos*'s interest in Schmitt was in some ways simply a continuation of previous work by George Schwab, Joseph Bendersky, and Ellen Kennedy, the new attention moved Schmitt's work more toward the center of intellectual debates; Jacques Derrida famously held up the two 1987 Schmitt *Telos* issues in his seminars in order to exhort the participants to take Schmitt seriously. Thus, the topics broached by Schmitt's work and brought to the attention of a wider scholarly audience by *Telos* signaled an evolution in the intellectual concerns of left-wing academic circles as well. Indeed, Schmitt's Shakespeare essay has long enjoyed a strong reception in Italy; in 1983, Simona Forti translated the text into Italian, with an introduction by the eminent legal philosopher Carlo Galli. Translations into French and Spanish followed in 1992 and 1993, and a "pirated" (and truncated) English translation was published in 2006. So this full translation of *Hamlet or Hecuba* into English, authorized by George Schwab and the Klett-Cotta Verlag, is long overdue. In the intervening 22 years, it has become more generally recognized that Schmitt's work is worthy of study and has the potential to reorient our thinking toward issues, such as decisionism, the friend-enemy distinction, the state of exception, and political representation, that were not considered worthy of discussion as concepts in the early 1980s but have now become very relevant.

Fittingly, this volume is the result of collaboration between myself and two Shakespeare scholars, whose interests in Schmitt concern the vexed exchanges among literature, politics, and theology in both the early modern and the modern periods. The appearance of this volume is due in large part to their initiative and efforts. Jennifer Rust nurtured the original idea for the volume. She was originally inspired to engage with Schmitt's *Hamlet* book through earlier work on *The Origin of German Tragic Drama* by Schmitt's interlocutor, Walter Benjamin. As a graduate student, she devoted herself to much of the "heavy lifting" of translating the rest of Schmitt's book before seeking me out as a collaborator. Julia Lupton guided and encouraged the project throughout. Their careful introduction chronicles the paths by which Schmitt's work has become essential reading for scholars who seek to understand the underlying political and cultural changes that made up the transition from the medieval to the modern period as well as the formative role of Renaissance texts in contemporary critical theory. While this introduction makes the case for the interdisciplinary significance of Schmitt's work, it also reflects on how the tragedy of Hamlet itself reveals certain tragic blind spots in Schmitt's own history and thought. My own commentary in the Afterword considers *Hamlet or Hecuba* in the context of Schmitt's ideas on political representation.

In spite of its anomalous position as a work of literary criticism in his oeuvre, this book speaks to the central and often unresolved problems of Schmitt's work. His reliance on tradition rather than reason as the basis of social order defines him as a conservative along the lines of Edmund Burke, Johann Georg Hamann, and Juan Donoso Cortés, and Schmitt extends this perspective by analyzing in *Hamlet or Hecuba* the representations linking the sovereign to the theater audience, and thus political forms to a popular will. Though the resulting theory of myth and politics conjures up visions of fascism and demagoguery, Schmitt's attempt to understand the mechanisms by which tragedy and myth originate lays out the starting points for making sense of both the cultural traditions and the modern political movements that have contributed to instances of the merging of democratic with religious, or pseudo-religious, elements. Schmitt's meditation on the links between literature and politics addresses then the mythic forms of political will formation that have unexpectedly come to determine both 20th and 21st century cultural and political history. If we live in a world that is no longer dominated by Europe and the West, but has been marked by conflicts and compromises between disparate cultures with diverging traditions, Schmitt's attack on the West's appeal to reason as an alibi for colonial domination resonates with a post-colonial critique, and his analysis of the origins of the Hamlet myth serves as part of a history of the mythic foundations of English colonialism. If his approach also recalls a kind of Nazi anti-colonialism and critique of the "West," then we should remain mindful of both the necessity and the danger of this critique for establishing grounds for cooperation in the world that has opened up before us, where political decisions are once again, as in Shakespeare's England, often driven by theological considerations as much as by material ones.

Yet, in spite of the political and religious conflicts that Schmitt's book analyzes, this volume seeks to continue a process of cultural mediation, first, in which Schmitt represented *Hamlet* to a German-speaking audience, and, second, in which the 1987 *Telos* issues sought to make his efforts relevant to an English-speaking one. If our current political conflicts often revolve around the kinds of cultural clashes that Schmitt imagines in his idea of the enemy, hopefully this volume will help bring his work to the attention of a broader audience and facilitate the mediation that is to be expected of a project of translation.

# TRANSLATORS' ACKNOWLEDGEMENTS

We would like to acknowledge the Klett-Cotta Verlag, which graciously granted the English language rights to the text, and the International Center for Writing and Translation at the University of California, Irvine, whose translation grant program made this publication possible. In addition, Saint Louis University provided a Summer Research Award and a Mellon Faculty Development grant that allowed us to complete the final stages of the translation in California, and the Alexander von Humboldt Foundation supported our work through their fellowship program. We are indebted to Julia Reinhard Lupton and Jane O. Newman, whose conscientious and tireless help, advice, and encouragement during the translation process was invaluable. We would also like to thank Wolfgang Iser, Ulrich Joost, Grant Kaplan, George Schwab, and Gary Ulmen for the time they devoted to reviewing the translation and their advice on specific translation difficulties. Jacques Derrida, Richard Halpern, Victoria Kahn, Rachel Porter, Ann Marie Rasmussen, Eric Santner, Adam Sitze, and Johannes Türk provided inspiration and encouragement at various stages of the project. Nicole Burgoyne, Jake Davis, and Dana Norwood deserve our thanks for their help with copy editing and the final layout, and we would like to acknowledge Brendan Bathrick for his superb cover design. Russell Berman, Tim Luke, and Mary Piccone at Telos Press Publishing provided editorial support for this project, and we are grateful for their help in seeing it through to completion. Finally, the work on this translation was initially inspired by Paul Piccone's vision and generosity.

# Introduction:
## Schmitt and Shakespeare

Jennifer R. Rust and Julia Reinhard Lupton

## 1. Carl Schmitt's Renaissance

The writings of Carl Schmitt have undergone a "renaissance" in the English-speaking world. Thrown into partial oblivion by the scandal of his affiliation with the Nazi party, Schmitt's most important works, *Political Theology: Four Chapters on the Concept of Sovereignty* (1922) and *The Concept of the Political* (1932), were finally translated into English in the 1980s.[1] Meanwhile, Schmitt's

1. *Political Theology: Four Chapters on Sovereignty*, trans. George Schwab (Cambridge, MA: MIT Press, 1985); *The Concept of the Political*, trans. George Schwab, was first published by MIT Press in 1985, and then re-released by the University of Chicago Press with a new Foreword by Tracy Strong in 1996. Other Schmitt titles published by MIT include *Political Romanticism*, trans. Guy Oakes (1986) and *The Crisis of Parliamentary Democracy*, trans Ellen Kennedy (1985). In 1996, Greenwood Press published two important volumes by Schmitt in English translation: *The Leviathan in the State Theory of Thomas Hobbes*, trans. George Schwab and Erna Hilfstein, and *Roman Catholicism and Political Form*, trans. G. L. Ulmen. Duke University Press published *Legality and Legitimacy*, trans. Jeffrey Seitzer, and with an introduction by John P. McCormick in 2004. *Der Begriff des Politischen* was reprinted in German in 1979, and *Politische Theologie* in 1970 and 1996 (Munich and Berlin: Duncker & Humblot). Finally, the translation of Schmitt's major postwar work, *The Nomos of the Earth in the International Law of the Jus Publicum Europaeum*, trans. G. L. Ulmen (New York: Telos Press Publishing, 2003), a text that considers the history of sovereignty in relation to changing spa-

correspondence with Walter Benjamin, as well as Benjamin's use
of Schmitt in *The Origin of German Tragic Drama,* have spurred
literary commentary by Samuel Weber, Giorgio Agamben, and
Eric Santner among others.[2] Schmitt and Benjamin, along with
their contemporary, Ernst Kantorowitz, each investigated the
persistence of seemingly archaic forms of ritual, exegesis and
allegory within a modern political order founded on the neutralization and privatization of religion. The discourse of political
theology has helped contemporary readers discern similar interests among Schmitt's precursors, contemporaries, critics, and
rivals, including Friedrich Nietzsche, Franz Rosenzweig, Franz
Kafka, Sigmund Freud, and Hannah Arendt—thinkers who
engaged with the subjective and collective destinies of monothe-
ism under secularization from their own distinctive situations
as enunciators of modernity.[3] The renewed interest in Schmitt
stems from the intellectual power of his critique of liberalism,
his prescient analysis of the dangers of wars fought in the name

tial orderings in Europe and the New World, has provided English-speaking
scholars with a broader vision of Schmitt's legal, geopolitical, and political-
theological thinking.

2. Samuel Weber, "Taking Exception to Decision: Walter Benjamin and Carl
Schmitt," *Diacritics* 22.3/4 (Autumn-Winter 1992): pp. 5-18; Giorgio Agamben, *State of Exception,* trans. Kevin Attell (Chicago: University of Chicago
Press, 2005); Eric Santner, *On Creaturely Life: Rilke, Benjamin, Sebald* (Chicago: University of Chicago Press, 2006). See as well Jacques Derrida, *The
Politics of Friendship,* trans. George Collins (London: Verso, 1997). From a
different angle, the essays collected by Chantal Mouffe under the title *The
Challenge of Carl Schmitt* (London: Verso, 1999) announced the possible rap-
prochement between Schmitt's polemically conservative thought and thinkers
on the Left in pursuit of alternatives to liberalism.

3. On Schmitt and Arendt, see Hans Sluga, "The Pluralism of the Political:
From Carl Schmitt to Hannah Arendt,"*Telos* 142 (Spring 2008): pp. 91-109.
For Schmitt, Freud, and Rosenzweig, see Eric Santner, *On the Psychotheology
of Everyday Life: Reflections on Freud and Rosenzweig* (Chicago: University of
Chicago Press, 2001); and Slavoj Zizek, Eric L. Santner, and Kenneth Reinhard, *The Neighbor: Three Inquiries in Political Theology* (Chicago: University
of Chicago Press, 2005).

of peace, his theorization of the state of emergency and the sovereign decision, and his insistence on the theological dimensions of sovereignty—ideas whose suspect pedigree has been made more palatable, as Tracy Strong suggests, by the receding memory of the Nazi period itself.[4] It is this very recession of Schmitt's historical context, however, that has also enabled the uncritical appropriation on the Right of some of these ideas in twenty-first century America, a trend that lends an immediate urgency to the current critical reappraisal of Schmitt's thought.[5]

In literary studies, the phrase "political theology" has come to designate the common sources and affiliations shared by politics and religion, as well as their antagonisms and internal resistances.[6] In Renaissance and early modern studies, "political theology" unites scholars who aim to develop some of the texts and impulses associated with critical theory in a direction defined by secularization, sovereignty, and biopower in the Renaissance and in contemporary life.[7] The phrase "political theology" itself

4. Strong, "Foreword: Dimensions of the New Debate around Carl Schmitt," in *The Concept of the Political*, by Carl Schmitt, p. xxvii.

5. The Bush Administration's efforts to expand executive power in the wake of the "state of emergency" declared after the terrorist attacks of September 11, 2001, revealed traces of the influence of a crude interpretation of Schmitt's thinking. For more extended analysis of the pertinence of Schmitt's theories to the American "War on Terror," see Agamben, *State of Exception*.

6. For a broader view of the scope of conceptual engagements with the topic of "political theology" across philosophy, psychoanalysis, religious studies, and political theory, see two recent edited collections by Hent de Vries and Lawrence E. Sullivan, *Political Theologies: Public Religions in a Post-Secular World* (New York: Fordham University Press, 2006); and Creston Davis, John Milbank and Slavoj Zizek, *Theology and the Political: The New Debate* (Durham: Duke University Press, 2005).

7. Renaissance scholars working in this area include Matthew Biberman, Kathleen Biddick, Paul Cefalu, Alice Dailey, Lowell Gallagher, Graham Hammill, Richard Halpern, Anselm Haverkamp, Victoria Kahn, Gregory Kneidel, James Kuzner, Ken Jackson, Jacques Lezra, Nichole Miller, Philip Lorenz, as well as the authors of this essay. See the review essay by Jackson and Marotti

has its origins in medieval iconographies of sacred kingship as distributed and displayed in the political, dramatic, and artistic forms of European civilization, along with the critique of traditional sovereignty mounted by Hobbes, Spinoza, Locke, and others in the seventeenth century; there is thus a special relationship between political theology as a critical approach to literature, politics, and thought and early modernity as a period and area of study.[8] The writings of Giorgio Agamben, the Italian translator of Walter Benjamin, have done much to integrate many

"The Religious Turn in Early Modern Studies," *Criticism* 46 (Winter 2004): pp. 167- 190; the special issue of *Religion and Literature* 38.3 (Autumn 2006), ed. Graham Hammill and Julia Reinhard Lupton, on "Sovereigns, Citizens, and Saints"; and the Cluster edited by Philip Lorenz, Issue edited by Bruce Holsinger, "The Religious Turn (to Theory) in Shakespeare Studies," *English Language Notes* (2006): pp. 145-48.

8. For Renaissance scholars, political theology is associated as much with Schmitt's contemporary, Ernst Kantorowicz, as it is with Schmitt. The subtitle of Ernst Kantorowicz's classic work, *The King's Two Bodies* (Princeton, NJ: Princeton University Press, 1957) is "A Study of Medieval Political Theology," prompting scholars in recent years to query the possible connections between Schmitt and Kantorowicz. Marie Axton has explored the significance of the concept of the ruler's two bodies during the reign of Elizabeth, when it was deployed to assuage anxieties provoked by the reign of a female monarch: *The Queen's Two Bodies: Drama and the Elizabethan Succession* (London: Royal Historical Society, 1977). Sergio Bertelli extends Kantorowicz's interest in the sacred character of pre-modern monarchy by examining a range of early modern and medieval rituals of kingship: *The King's Body: Sacred Rituals of Power in Medieval and Early Modern Europe*, trans. R. Burr Litchfield (University Park: University of Pennsylvania Press, 2001). On the negative side, David Norbrook, Richard Hardin, and Lorna Hutson have offered critiques that question the politics and historical accuracy of Kantorowicz's account of the prevalence of the "two bodies" doctrine in early modern England. See Norbrook, "The Emperor's New Body? *Richard II*, Ernst Kantorowicz, and the Politics of Shakespeare Criticism," *Textual Practice* 10.2 (1996): pp. 329-357; Hutson, "Not the King's Two Bodies: Reading the Body Politic in Shakespeare's *Henry IV.*" *Rhetoric and Law in Early Modern Europe*, ed. Lorna Hutson and Victoria Kahn (New Haven: Yale University Press, 2001): pp. 166-189; Hardin, *Civil Idolatry: Desacralizing and Monarchy in Spenser, Shakespeare, and Milton* (Newark: University of Delaware Press, 1992).

concerns and motifs derived from Schmitt into a framework that takes its starting point far to the left of Schmitt's own thinking: in the environs of Foucault, and in the line of Italian Marxists concerned with different figurations of the multitude in political thought after Machiavelli.[9] Reading Schmitt in relationship to Jewish Messianism, Foucauldian biopolitics, and Italian political thought, Agamben recasts political theology in a framework both oriented towards the historical scenes of early modernity and attentive to the afterlife of Renaissance and Baroque motifs in later literary and political formations.

This introduction places Schmitt's thoughts on *Hamlet* in the context of current developments in Renaissance studies. Although we take issue with the literary and political *teloi* of Schmitt's *Hamlet*-interpretation, his staging of the relationship between literature and history anticipates later developments in literary criticism, including psychoanalysis and the new historicism. Whether or not readers agree with Schmitt's sometimes blunt allegorical reading of *Hamlet*, access to the full text of *Hamlet or Hecuba* in English should provide crucial new materials for scholars interested in expanding, defining, and critiquing

9. See especially *Homo Sacer: Sovereign Power and Bare Life*, trans. Daniel Heller-Roazen (Stanford: Stanford University Press, 1998), but also Agamben's analysis of Messianism in *The Time That Remains: A Commentary on the Letter to the Romans*, trans. Patricia Dailey (Stanford: Stanford University Press, 2005), and the recent collection, *Giorgio Agamben: Sovereignty and Life*, ed. Matthew Calarco and Steven DeCaroli (Stanford: Stanford University Press, 2007), which includes a short essay by Agamben on the life of the multitude from Aristotle to Dante. On the multitude in Italian political thought, see especially *Multitude: War and Democracy in the Age of Empire* (New York: Penguin Press, 2004), by Michael Hardt and Antonio Negri. Eric Santner's *On the Psychotheology of Everyday Life* and *On Creaturely Life* have done much to create links among political theology (with its conservative and often Christian genealogy), psychoanalysis, and Jewish philosophy around questions of life. David Pan takes issue with Agamben's reading of Schmitt: "Carl Schmitt on Culture and Violence in the Political Decision," *Telos* 142 (Spring 2008): pp. 49 -72.

the aims of political theology as a particular way of approaching literature, theory, and politics. We begin by reviewing several recent engagements with Schmitt's book by critics writing in English as an entrance into considering how Schmitt's historical reading of *Hamlet* responds to the provocation of Walter Benjamin's more celebrated *The Origin of German Tragic Drama*. In the next section, we frame Schmitt's identification of Hamlet as a myth born of religious schism with reference to the development of Schmitt's concept of political representation in his early book, *Roman Catholicism and Political Form* (1923). We end by connecting certain themes in *Hamlet or Hecuba* with the argument of Schmitt's major post-war book, *Nomos of the Earth* (1950). It is our contention throughout this Introduction that *Hamlet or Hecuba* demonstrates the essential role that Renaissance and Baroque literature and thought have played in the pre- and post-histories of political theology as a distinctive method and debate uniting diverse practitioners in the humanities today.

## 2. *Hamlet*'s Exception: Schmitt's "Source of the Tragic"

Schmitt published his *Hamlet* essay in 1956 after leading a seminar on the topic at the Volkshochschule in Düsseldorf the year before; it was later translated into French and Italian, the latter under the auspices of the prominent legal philosopher Carlo Galli, who wrote a bracing and revelatory introduction to the text. At the core of *Hamlet or Hecuba* is Schmitt's argument that Hamlet's inhibitions and the uncertainty concerning Gertrude's guilt reflect the situation of James I, in particular the murder of his father, Lord Darnley, in 1566 and the subsequent "o'erhasty" marriage of his mother, Mary Queen of Scots, to the murderer. Distinguishing his method from both the subjectivism of Romantic and Freudian readings and the objectivism of a strictly historical approach, Schmitt proposes to answer instead "the question of the source of the tragic action as such" (p. 10).[10] And the source of the tragic, it turns out, comes from the special relationship between reality and poetry that obtains when, as in *Hamlet*, a traumatic historical scandal meets up with literary materials, creating ambiguities and disturbances with the capacity to raise the work of art into a state of exception with regard to traditional genres such as revenge tragedy or Senecan drama.

The title phrase "Hamlet or Hecuba" refers to Hamlet's third soliloquy, when the Prince responds to the theatrical virtuosity of the Player's Speech with a declamation decrying his own inadequacy. Schmitt prefers to quote the speech from the First or so-called "Bad" Quarto of 1603 (p. 43, note 31); here, we cite it from the Second Quarto of 1604-1605:

> O what a rogue and pesant slaue am I.
> Is it not monstrous that this player heere
> But in a fixion, in a dreame of passion
> Could force his soule so to his owne conceit
> That from her working all the visage wand,
> Teares in his eyes, distraction in his aspect,
> A broken voyce, an his whole function suting
> With formes to his conceit; and all for nothing,
> For *Hecuba*.
> What's *Hecuba* to him, or he to her,
> That he should weepe for her? what would he doe
> Had he the motiue, and that for passion
> That I haue?[11]

---

10. Page numbers in parentheses throughout the text refer to the translation of *Hamlet or Hecuba* in this volume.

11. William Shakespeare, *The tragicall historie of Hamlet, Prince of Denmarke* (London: James Roberts for Nicholas Ling, 1604), ll. 1590-1602. Schmitt prefers the First Quarto of 1603, also known as the "Bad Quarto"—*The tragicall historie of Hamlet Prince of Denmarke by William Shake-speare* (London: Valentine Simmes for Nicholas Ling and Iohn Trundell, 1603)—published *before* James's succession to the throne, because he argues that Hamlet's ambitions to rule are clearer, mirroring the interest of the Essex circle in James's claims to the throne. Modern editors attribute most of these variations not to revision or censorship, but to the poor textual state of the First Quarto, likely a "memorial

Schmitt associates the Player's tears for Hecuba with the clas-
sicizing world of a continental theatre already shaped by the
lineaments of the modern state. Hamlet's inability to weep for
Hecuba—that is, for a character who bears no immediate relationship to his own situation—indicates for Schmitt the concreteness
and immediacy of the Elizabethan stage, in which history, representation and life interpenetrate, sometimes painfully, without
the mediating circuits of pure play (*Spiel*) that would sublimate
theatre into a space distinct from that of the spectators. For
Schmitt, the possibility of empathy implies also the insertion of
an aesthetic distance. Hamlet, writes Schmitt, "does not weep for
Hecuba" (p. 42); so, too, we spectators of the play are not "meant
to weep for Hamlet as the actor wept for the Trojan queen. We
would, however, in point of fact weep for Hamlet as for Hecuba
if we wished to divorce the reality of our present existence from
the play on the stage" (p. 43).[12] According to Schmitt, the his-

reconstruction" by an actor. J. Dover Wilson, one of the major Shakespearean critics of the early twentieth century with whom Schmitt is constantly
in dialogue throughout *Hamlet or Hecuba,* dismisses the First Quarto as "a
garbled text based upon notes got together by someone, whether actor or
spectator, present at original performances of the play, as all critics are now
agreed" (*What Happens in Hamlet* [Cambridge, UK: Cambridge University
Press, 1951], p. 120). The version of *Hamlet* that we are accustomed to reading today is usually a conflation of the texts of the Second Quarto (1604-05)
and the First Folio (1623). For a thorough account of the complicated history
of the critical reception of the varying texts of *Hamlet,* see Leah Marcus, "Bad
Taste and Bad Hamlet," in *Unediting the Renaissance: Shakespeare, Marlowe,
Milton* (New York: Routledge, 1996). From a New Historicist perspective,
Marcus also defends the value of the "Bad Quarto" although on very different
grounds than those claimed by Schmitt. She seeks to "recast the discussion
about Q1 *Hamlet* entirely by considering that text and its 'betters' in terms of
the differing expectations created by orality and writing as competing forms
of communication within the Renaissance playhouse," p. 137. The different
Quartos and the Folio can be compared at http://internetshakespeare.uvic.ca/
Library/plays/Ham.html (accessed 8/16/2008).

12. Johannes Türk points out that the phrase itself was common in Germany.
In a speech of 1887, Bismarck said of public protests over the independence

tory of drama is split between the reflective self-containment of *Trauerspiel* and the authenticity of tragedy, which comes into being when the playwright allows his fictions to be broken up by historical time, understood not as the normative "forms and pressures" of historical context, but rather as the kind of scandal or breach represented by the family romance of James.

Schmitt's analysis of tragedy as the incursion of historical time into the illusion of aesthetic unity may seem naïve or essentialist, too candidly invested in a simple division between art and history, text and context. By extension, the reading of *Hamlet* pursued by Schmitt often feels tendentious and even amateurish, blinkered and retarded by Schmitt's fixation on the Hamlet-James couple. In the most extended reading to date of *Hamlet or Hecuba* executed from within Renaissance studies, Victoria Kahn argues that Schmitt disavows the aesthetic because he associates it with the liberal neutralization of politics that occurred throughout the eighteenth and nineteenth centuries.[13] The aesthetic in this sense is the corollary of the rise of representative parliamentary democracy with which Schmitt became so disenchanted during the Weimar period. Although Kahn grants some value to Schmitt's "efforts to read Shakespearean tragedy in the context of the historical shift from medieval theology to the secular nation state," his analysis rests in Kahn's view on an untenable opposition between "real action" and "mere literary invention."[14] In his vigorous response to Kahn and other critics who have tried to

of Bulgaria, "When I first read these declamations—they are partly whining, partly pathetic—I could not help being reminded of the scene from 'Hamlet,' in which the actor declaims and sheds tears over the destiny of Hecuba—real tears—and Hamlet says ... 'What's Hecuba to him?' .... What is Bulgaria to us?" Otto von Bismark, January 11, 1887; cited Johannes Türk, "The Intrusion: Carl Schmitt's Non-Mimetic Logic of Art," *Telos* 142 (Spring 2008): p. 88.

13. Victoria Kahn, "Hamlet or Hecuba: Carl Schmitt's Decision," *Representations* 83 (Summer, 2003): p. 69.

14. Ibid., pp. 84-85.

reduce Schmitt's argument to a simple choice between the real and the representational, to Hamlet *or* Hecuba, Johannes Türk insists that Schmitt does not simply oppose the aesthetic and the political, but rather posits the aesthetic as the "non-mimetic" site for displaying the *difference between* politics and aesthetics.[15] For Schmitt, the political emerges as the tragic only insofar as it deforms the aesthetic, which becomes nothing more nor less than the record of its own deviation from pure play. Contrary to the claim that Schmitt has "nothing of substance to say about the 'public sphere' in which Shakespeare's dramas were performed,"[16] Türk finds that Schmitt posits a collective "political" unconscious that draws upon the structures of "condensations and displacements" (*Verdichtungen und Verschiebungen*) of Freud's dream-work (p. 36).[17] In this regard, Schmitt is not far from the project of Freud's *Totem and Taboo* in seeking to delineate the mechanisms and structures of a collective political psyche, even if he differs in certain particulars.[18] According to Türk, Schmitt's account of tragedy is precisely not "positivistic,"[19] but attentive to the political as the negative within the aesthetic.[20]

In his introduction to the Italian edition, Carlo Galli argues that Schmitt's Hamlet presents not a myth of origins but a figure of fissure, who, at the level of collective memory, records and bears witness to the fractures caused by religious civil war and shifting geopolitical orientation suffered by Europe in the seventeenth century and still ongoing in their effects today.[21] Adam

15. Türk, pp. 74-89.

16. Kahn, p. 87.

17. Quoted in Türk, p. 82.

18. Ibid., p. 80.

19. Kahn, p. 84.

20. Türk, pp. 87-88.

21. Carlo Galli, "Presentazione dell'Edizione Italiana," in *Amleto o Ecuba: L'Irrompere del Tempo nel Gioco del Dramma*, by Carl Schmitt, trans. Simona Forti (Bologna: Il Mulino, 1983), p. 34.

Sitze, following the train of thought initiated by Galli, identifies originary conflict (*polemos*) as the core of Schmitt's definition of the tragic, and he does so in order to demonstrate both the tragic parameters of Schmitt's thinking as such, and the importance of *Hamlet or Hecuba* to understanding Schmitt's larger project. "Tragic conflictuality," argues Sitze, "is not merely Schmitt's *object of knowledge,* the silent paradigm for his concept of the political. It is the innermost kernel—the divided origin—of *his own political thought.*"[22] It is this element of conflict, Galli, Türk and Sitze suggest, that gives any instance of concrete reality the stealth and power of an intruder.

This negative operation of historical time is evident in the most powerful example of literary reading in Schmitt's essay:

> [*Hamlet*] has two major openings through which historical time breaks into [*einbricht*] the time of the play . . . Both intrusions—the taboo surrounding the guilt of the queen, and the distortion of the avenger that leads to the Hamletization of the hero—are shadows, two dark areas. They are in no sense mere historical-political connections, neither simple allusions [*Anspielungen*] nor true mirrorings [*Spiegelungen*], but rather two given circumstances [*Gegebenheiten*] that are received and respected by the play and around which the play timidly maneuvers. They disturb the unintentional character of pure play and, in this respect, are a *minus*. Nevertheless, they made it possible for the figure of Hamlet to become a true myth. In this respect they are a *plus,* because they succeeded in elevating *Trauerspiel* to tragedy. (p. 44)

Schmitt distinguishes the negative force of the intrusion from the minor historical impress of mere "allusions or true mirrorings" (p. 35) by virtue of its intimate yet dangerous association with the "realities" of the actual sovereign figure (p. 48). The *minus* or negative space of these intrusions becomes a *plus* insofar as

---

22. Adam Sitze, "A Space without War, a War without Space: Remarks on the Juridical and Political Thought of Carlo Galli," unpublished essay; cited with permission of the author.

they interrupt the pure "*Spiel*" of the *Trauerspiel* with the "tragic" weight of genuine historicity, a weight that becomes a void with the passage of time, a cryptic cipher continually refilled by philosophical or psychoanalytic speculation. The *Einbruch*, in short, functions as an *exception* to the normative order of representation that, far from damaging the play, intensifies its dramatic effect. Like the sovereign's decision, the intrusion of real time into the play of representation functions as a creation *ex nihilo*, inserting a negative space into the drama around which new forms of imaginative encounter can take place. The "time" of the essay's subtitle is not a positive content reflected by the play in the manner of a representation, but rather a negative quotient—a "surplus value" (p. 45), "the shadow of objective reality" (p. 52) that interrupts the play as precisely what cannot be directly depicted in it.

Despite Schmitt's overt disavowals of the classic psychoanalytic account of *Hamlet*, passages like this, with their explicit concern with familiacide, incest, and the formal techniques and symptoms of repression in response to real trauma, echo psychoanalytic methods of reading. Moreover, Schmitt's emphasis on the guilt of the mother reflects features of the negative Oedipus complex, which he actually names in several places (pp. 7; 51). Although Freud is the most immediate reference point for a psychoanalytic account of Schmitt, his discussions of the real and of creation *ex nihilo* anticipate aspects of Lacan. For Schmitt, unlike Freud, the repressed lies not in the unconscious infantile desires of the author's individual psyche, but rather in the "concrete" historical reality of a political taboo. This reality appears in the drama not directly, but through a glass darkly, as an opacity interrupting the surface of pure, purposeless play.[23] Schmitt's

23. The Freudian references also invite comparison between Schmitt's repression of repression and the more direct engagement with psychoanalysis pursued by his contemporary and rival, the liberal jurist Hans Kelsen, a friend of Freud who contributed an essay on group psychology and legal theory to Freud's journals in 1922 (in German) and 1924 (revised in English). See Hans

emphasis on the radical intrusion of time in the play powerfully evokes modes of historicity that carry the deforming impact of trauma and taboo, and thus challenges simple contextualization without rejecting history as an appropriate frame for interpreting literature.

Kenneth Reinhard compares Schmitt's sovereign to the primal father in Freud: "The primal father and the sovereign occupy the position of extreme dictators whose word both violates the rule of the total state and promises it *totality*, closure, drawing the line between the inside and the outside."[24] Reinhard urges the necessity of supplementing Schmitt's political theology of the sovereign with a more horizontal political theology of the neighbour. Whether we read the real in Schmitt as a naïve and vitalist essentialism (as Kahn does) or (following Galli, Türk, and Sitze) as a more existential and conflictual nihilism—and surely both are tendencies in this text—the real remains the source of the tragic in Schmitt's reading of the play. Our own account pursues the existential and conflictual paths opened by Türk, Galli, and Sitze, but we concur with Kahn that elements of vitalism continue to dog this troubling text, and we agree with Reinhard that Schmitt's oeuvre requires a broader engagement with anti-sovereign moments in his writing. Schmitt's dialogue with Benjamin constitutes a productive arena for exploring these tensions and potentialities.

Kelsen, "The Conception of the State and Social Psychology—With Special Reference to Freud's Group Theory," *International Journal of Psycho-Analysis* 5 (1924): 1-38; and commentary by Julia Reinhard Lupton, "Invitation to a Totem Meal: Hans Kelsen and Political Theology," unpublished essay, (submitted for the volume, *Tarrying with the Subjunctive: The Return of Theory in Early Modern Studies*, ed. Bryan Reynolds and Paul Cefalu; under consideration at Palgrave).

24. Reinhard, p. 56.

## 3. The Sovereign and the Creature: Schmitt and Benjamin

In *The Origin of German Tragic Drama* (1927), Benjamin uses Schmitt's magisterial announcement from *Political Theology*— "Sovereign is he who decides the exception."[25]—to gloss the world of Baroque tragedy. In *Political Theology*, Schmitt posits the *Ausnahmezustand* (state of exception or emergency) as that condition in which an extralegal act—the exception to the rule of law—serves to support and re-establish a constitutional order in crisis, through the cut of the sovereign's decision. Schmitt compares the decision of the sovereign to God's creation of the world *ex nihilo*: "That constitutive, specific element of a decision is, from the perspective of the underlying norm, new and alien. Looked at normatively, the decision emanates from nothingness."[26] Benjamin implicitly challenges Schmitt's comparison when he writes: "Whereas the modern concept of sovereignty amounts to a supreme executive power on the part of the prince, the baroque concept emerges from a discussion of the state of emergency [*Ausnahmezustand*], and makes it the most important function of the prince to avert this."[27] Benjamin both incorporates and severely limits Schmitt's definition of sovereignty by marking the irreducible difference that haunts Schmitt's insistent attempts to concretize the analogy between the sovereign and God. Unlike God, the sovereign of Baroque *Trauerspiel* is mired in a radical immanence that permits no transcendence, no *aura* of sacred presence: "However highly he is enthroned over subject and state, his status is confined to the world of creation; he is the lord of creatures, but he remains a creature."[28] The createdness of the creaturely sovereign ruins his capacity to command

25. Schmitt, *Political Theology*, p. 5.

26. Ibid., pp. 31-32.

27. Benjamin's footnote is to Schmitt, *Politische Theologie*, which he cites several times. Walter Benjamin, *The Origin of German Tragic Drama*, trans. John Osborne (London: New Left Books, 1977), p. 65.

28. Benjamin, *The Origin of German Tragic Drama*, p. 85.

the force of the genuine exception. The creaturely sovereign is unable to achieve the authentic breakthrough, the "miraculous" decision; he is condemned to indecision and self-destruction since the difference between the exceptional case of the state of emergency and the norm can no longer be discerned. As Samuel Weber argues, on Benjamin's Baroque stage, the sovereign figure is both hollowed out and fragmented, split off into the multiple personas of the tyrant, the martyr, and the Intrigant.[29]

In *Hamlet or Hecuba*, written decades after both *Political Theology* and *The Origin of German Tragic Drama*, Schmitt reopens the dialogue with Walter Benjamin, retracing his steps through the play that Benjamin had put forward as the exemplary instance of the melancholic martyrology of the Baroque *Trauerspiel:* "Only in a princely life such as this is melancholy redeemed in being confronted with itself."[30] Schmitt responds to Benjamin's account of the Baroque sovereign by repeating Benjamin's strategy of misappropriation and inversion, turning the earlier technique of his friend-enemy to his own ends. Schmitt's own treatment of *Hamlet* accepts many of Benjamin's premises, only in order to overturn his conclusions in a reading that seeks to restore some of the vitality that Benjamin evacuates from the spectacle of Baroque sovereignty. This strategy is especially evident in the question of the play within the play [*Spiel im Spiel*], the theatrical convention which, for both Schmitt and Benjamin, functions as an *exceptional* time and space within the theater of sovereignty, a point of rupture that illustrates the fundamental difference between seventeenth century drama and the Aristotelian unities. For both, the exceptional instance of the play within the play proves the rule of the representation of sovereignty in the drama at large. This rule of theatrical representation also provides a key to grasping the nature of European sovereignty

29. Weber, "Taking Exception to Decision," pp. 14-5.
30. Benjamin, *The Origin of German Tragic Drama*, p. 158.

itself at a time in which, to paraphrase the lines from Lohenstein quoted by both Schmitt and Benjamin, play and theater [*Spiel und Schauplatz*] are inextricably intertwined with "the life of those whose element is the court" (p. 41).[31]

While Schmitt agrees that this formulation is apt for the period, he makes an effort to distinguish the exceptional case of Shakespeare's England from the artificial order of the continental state. The inauthentic character of the "baroque theatricalization of life" on the continent must be contrasted with the raw force of the living theater of Shakespeare's time and place: "[A]s primal theater it was all the more intensely integrated into its current reality, a part of the present [*ein Stück Gegenwart*] in a society that largely perceived its own action as theater—a theater which consequently did not set up an opposition between the present of the play and the lived actuality of a contemporary present" (p. 41). Shakespeare's dramas emerge from an "elementary" milieu unconscious of any strict distinction between the theater of life and the life of the theatre, a milieu not "civilized" [*poliziert*] (p. 47) in the sense that developed in the European continent later in the seventeenth century. We further address Schmitt's specific concept of this phase of English history in the final section of this essay, but for now, it is important to note that for Schmitt *Hamlet* participates in the "lived actuality" of Shakespeare's era to such an extent that it appears nearly identical with this historical present, a "part," literally a "piece" or "play" [*Stück*] of immediate historical presence.

Thanks to this vital continuity between the theatricality of Shakespeare's historical moment and the stage, the royal figure of Shakespeare's drama, rather than presenting a hollow and fragmented image of "creaturely" sovereignty, makes contact with the person of a real sovereign. In the case of *Hamlet*, the sov-

---

31. Ibid., pp. 92-93; Walter Benjamin, *Der Ursprung des deutschen Trauerspiels* (Frankfurt: Suhrkamp, 1955), p. 271.

ereign presence woven into the theatrical spectacle belongs to James I, the King of Scotland who ascended to the English throne in 1603, two years after the first performances of the drama. In Schmitt's reading, Shakespeare superimposes the traditional persona of the revenge hero onto the actual personality of the living monarch, who would have endowed this mask with a particular significance for the intuitive observer of the time. Schmitt asserts that for Shakespeare's original audience, "behind the stage figure Hamlet, another figure has remained standing. The spectators of that time also saw this figure when they saw Hamlet" (pp. 20-21). The sovereign and the stage figure originally supplemented each other in an "elemental" (p. 48) dynamic proper to the English "public sphere" (p. 35).

While the double figure of "Hamlet-James" may have been readily apparent to Shakespeare's contemporary audience, with the decay of this present context, the personality behind the mask loses its immediacy and legibility, but nonetheless gains a peculiar, ghostly form of sovereignty, retaining the force of a negative presence embedded within the surrounding *Trauerspiel*. This negative presence actually becomes doubly sovereign: on one hand, it registers the trace of the presence of the historical sovereign barely concealed behind the stage mask, and, on the other, it transcends the ahistorical essence of the ordinary theatrical play by allowing history to "intrude" or break through the aesthetic norms of representation.

Schmitt finds confirmation for his hypothesis about the underlying connection between James and the "distorted" revenge hero of *Hamlet* in the exceptional case of "The Mousetrap," the play within the play of Act Three. In "The Mousetrap," which mirrors both the death of James's father and the question of his mother's complicity, the "intrusion" of history emerges as a metatheatrical exception to the aesthetic order of the stage play, a kind of special effect that constitutes a higher order of play that defies, but also defines, the conventions of ordinary play: "The play on stage could magnify itself as play without detaching itself from the immediate reality of life. . . . Here one can speak even of a triple magnification, because the preceding pantomime, the 'dumb show', once again mirrors the core of the tragic action" (pp. 41-42). The spectacular layering of theatrical effects amplifies rather than dilutes the potency of the sovereign presence that animates the play. The force of the present expands as it divides into multiple reflective surfaces, a tendency especially evident in the triplication of the meta-drama in "The Mousetrap." For Schmitt, this intensification of spectacle reveals the essential unity between the play and the historical sovereign: the play within the play "is not only no look *behind* the scenes [*hinter die Kulissen*], but, on the contrary, it is the real play repeated *before* the curtains [vor *den Kulissen*]" (p. 43, emphasis added). If the drama as a whole functions as a mask, an "*incognito*" (p. 37) for the sovereign James, then the play within the play, staging the primal scene of the murder of the father and the seduction of the mother by the murderer, the original crime that shapes the actual personality of James and the character of Hamlet as revenge hero, stands out as the moment when this mask slips off entirely.

Schmitt argues, then, that the triply mediated representation of the play within the play opens onto a revelation of the most unmediated historical reality. Schmitt asserts that the play within the play is "a consummate test of the hypothesis that a core of historical actuality and historical presence . . . has the power to intensify the play as play without destroying the sense of the tragic" (p. 44). The "tragic" signifies the irruption of real sovereign presence, under the sign, however, of taboo and scandal, into the play "before" the play, into the first-order play of the *Trauerspiel* that constitutes the greater part of *Hamlet*. Like the state of emergency in relation to constitutional norms, sovereign play is both included and excluded in the stage play, rendering the distinction between the two indeterminate. While the sovereign can become magnified through multiple reflective theatrical techniques, suggesting a persona that actively partakes in the "playful" artifice in which it is embedded, multiple layers of theatrical reflection cannot overwhelm the singularity of this "core" of an intrusive, negative presence. Mere play may endlessly reproduce and refract itself, but the core of historical scandal concerning the sovereignty of the king is not subject to this process of division and multiplication in the same sense: there can be no "tragedy within a tragedy" (p. 44). Transparent to the contemporary audience, yet all but invisible to the modern eye, this authentic tragic "core" does not disperse into the surrounding play.

In making this argument, Schmitt seeks to draw an opposite conclusion from a set of premises that nonetheless cannot be entirely separated from Benjamin's account of the baroque play within the play. Schmitt raises the spectre of an alternative version of the play within the play that bears a striking resemblance to Benjamin's argument in the subchapter of *The Origin of German Tragic Drama* entitled "Play and Reflection." Shakespeare's play within the play, Schmitt insists, necessarily "presupposes a realistic core of the most intense contemporary significance and timeliness" (pp. 43-44). Without such a potent core, "the doubling would simply make the play more playful, more unlikely and artificial . . . until finally it would become a 'parody of itself'" (p. 44). In the fallen world of Benjamin's baroque theater, lapsing into parody is an ever-present possibility because any true transcendence is impossible. The link between play and life in Benjamin's analysis resides in a common awareness of the discrepancy between the "creaturely" world and the divine world. Rather than naturalizing theater, a theological fixation on the *createdness of the creaturely* produces a theatricalization of nature, a nature denaturalized.[32] This situation threatens to incapacitate

32. On the creature as an immanent variation on political theology, see Julia Reinhard Lupton, "Creature Caliban," *Shakespeare Quarterly* 51, no. 1 (Spring 2000): pp. 1-23, for an elaboration of Jewish universalism in Shakespeare; and

the absolute sovereign who must emulate the decisive power of a transcendent God. The play within the play dissimulates a form of sovereign transcendence by means of creaturely devices. By virtue of its very artificiality, Benjamin claims, it represents an "indirect inclusion of transcendence—as it were mirrored, crystallized, or in marionette-form" in the midst of the otherwise quite worldly theater play.[33] If there is a moment of revelation in the play within the play for Benjamin, it is that of a *mise en abyme* of artifice in the place of authentic sovereignty.

While Schmitt may contest Benjamin's detachment of a "core" of transcendent sovereign presence from the artificial spectacle of the meta-drama which surrounds it, he nonetheless makes the provocative point that a certain *effect* of sovereign presence may be potentialized, intensified rather than diminished by the overlay of multiple modes of theatrical artifice. Moreover, to conceive of such intrusions as forms of exception implies a non-normative understanding of genre quite close to Benjamin's own. While Benjamin also gestures toward the possibility of a resurrection of transcendent sovereignty in the play within the play, his emphasis falls more on the creaturely mechanism which creates this effect rather than on the different possible *effectivities* of this effect, including the possibility that the sovereign may be "magnified" just as easily as "parodied" through spectacular media techniques.

Thus, to counter the creatureliness of Benjamin's baroque sovereign, Schmitt asserts a version of transcendence in *Hamlet* via a kind of negative political theology. Both Benjamin and Schmitt stage tragedy as an existential conflict between dramatic representation and forms of history that unfold under the sign of

Eric Santner, *On Creaturely Life*, for a post-Renaissance discussion of these themes. Galli comments on Benjamin's creature in the context of evaluating the Schmitt-Benjamin relationship, "Presentazione," p. 25.

33. Benjamin, *The Origin of German Tragic Drama*, p. 81; *Der Ursprung des deutschen Trauerspiels*, p. 260.

scandal, trauma, and loss, and both conceptualize that conflict as instituting a theological dimension. Benjamin's creaturely perspective is grounded, however, on the horizontal plane of a fallen nature swarming with a multitude of abjected beings defined by their loss of contact with the Creator but animated by Messianic anticipations. The motif of the creature, equal parts Golem and worm, supine life form and emergent technicity, is affiliated with the writings of Benjamin's contemporary, Franz Rosenzweig. The political theology of the creature represents a thinking of the universal pursued from within Judaism that counterbalances Schmittian political theology with a different set of themes, sources, and destinies. Schmitt, on the other hand, takes the analogy between the sovereign and the Creator rather than his status as a Creature as the orienting moment of the tragic situation. Schmitt attributes a peculiar sovereign force to the tabooed presence of a concrete historical trauma at the very center of the play. The sovereign, like God, creates *ex nihilo*—under a situation of duress, emergency and conflict—and this *nihil,* pocketed within tragedy as its mythic core, draws the limit of representational play.

## 4. Hamlet in Westphalia: Religious Schism and Political Representation in Schmitt's *Hamlet*

The figure of the historical James can certainly be taken, not without good reason, as an instance of Schmitt's romance with personal sovereignty. Yet the personality of James, if the object of a fierce and partisan attraction, itself always embodies a split for Schmitt. Baptized Catholic by his mother and raised by Protestants far away from her, the person of James represents for Schmitt "a king who in his fate and character was the product of the strife of his age" (p. 30), a man "literally from the womb immersed in the schisms of his era" (p. 27). James' own biography is a livid, living conflict, and it is only under the aspect of schism that his person—at once body, mask, and name—comes to insert an aesthetic conflict between historical reality and the play of representation into *The Tragicall Historie of Hamlet Prince of Denmarke*. Indeed, James becomes the site and symptom of the conflict within Schmitt's own writing between an extraordinary openness to the vicissitudes of literary form in history and an equally powerful narrowing down of the play's possible significations. Although Schmitt admired James I's writings on absolute monarchy, more is at stake here than Hamlet's cryptic identification with James; or rather, that identification opens onto a broader crisis in European politics and theology, the Reformation, an event corresponding for Schmitt with the emergence of the modern state.

In his "Results" [*Ergebnis*], which fall near the end of *Hamlet or Hecuba*, Schmitt writes that myths are born when time breaks into the play of representation: "[I]n distinguishing *Trauerspiel* and tragedy, we can recognize that incontrovertible core of a singular historical reality that transcends every subjective invention and can then understand its elevation to myth" (p. 53). Myths form, Schmitt claims, at the intersection of history and representation, at the moment when traumatic elements of the temporal order break into the norms established by authorial intentions and the conventions of genre. Put otherwise, *myth is literature's exception*, embodying the piece of historical reality that is in literature but more than literature, and hence drives specific artistic creations out of their historical periods in order to reach a more universal status.

One must approach the category of myth in Schmitt's thought with caution. Victoria Kahn cites a passage from Mussolini favored by Schmitt: "We have created a myth, this myth is a belief, a noble enthusiasm; it does not need to be a reality, it is a striving and a hope, belief, and courage. Our myth is the nation."[34] Certainly one arc of *Hamlet or Hecuba* is to present Hamlet as

34. Kahn, p.72.

such a myth: the myth of the sovereign behind the prince, the real presence of the king behind the actor on stage, and, by extension, the myth of sovereignty *as* presence. As we have suggested, Schmitt attempts to immunize the sovereign "core" of *Hamlet* from the danger of "self-parody" by reinstalling the authority of a living sovereign at the heart of Benjamin's Baroque hall of mirrors. Kahn claims that Schmitt ultimately seeks to portray *Hamlet* as a "counter-myth or antidote" to Hobbes' *Leviathan*; as Schmitt argues in his earlier essay on Catholicism and political form, "once the state becomes a leviathan, it disappears from the world of representation."[35] In the leviathan-state, particularly as Schmitt comes to understand it in his later work on Hobbes' "failed myth,"[36] authority is depersonalized, mechanized, in contrast to the personalization of sovereignty still legible in the reign of the Stuarts.

Nonetheless, the myth that Schmitt derives from Hamlet in the conclusion to his monograph embodies a division rather than shores up a unity. Schmitt writes that Renaissance poetry has yielded three great "symbolic figures": the Catholic Don Quixote, the Protestant Faust, and Hamlet, who "stands between them in the middle of the schism that has determined the fate of Europe" (p. 53). Of the three, only the schismatic Hamlet classifies as "already" a "myth." The schism in the midst of which the mythic Hamlet stands is, of course, the Reformation and the wars of religion that it spawned. The consequences of the Reformation loomed large in Schmitt's early development of the concept of "political theology," a project intertwined with his efforts to formulate a theory of Catholicism as "political form." Schmitt was born in Westphalia, into a Catholic family that

35. Schmitt, *Roman Catholicism and Political Form*, p. 21.

36. For this re-evaluation, see Carl Schmitt, *The Leviathan in the State Theory of Thomas Hobbes: Meaning and Failure of a Political Symbol*, trans. George Schwab and Erna Hilfstein (Chicago and London: University of Chicago Press, 2008).

resided in a Protestant town.[37] In central Europe, the Peace of
Westphalia, cemented by a series of treaties during the period
from 1648-1668, determined the borders of many of the modern European states, and affirmed the principle that each prince
would determine the religion of his state: cuius regio, eius religio.
In this crucial moment in the formation of the modern political
state, the sovereign becomes he who decides the religion of his
territory.

Grounded in this historical context, Schmitt's initial thinking of the political is marked by the lingering traces of the trauma
of confessional schism. In *Roman Catholicism and Political Form*
(1923), written in close proximity to *Political Theology* (1922)
and in dialogue with Weber's *Protestant Ethic and the Spirit of
Capitalism*,[38] Schmitt proposes the Roman Church as a reservoir
of political force in an increasingly technological and rational-
ized modern state. He accepts Weber's account of an intrinsic
link between Protestant spirituality and the rise of modern
capitalism, but emphasizes that this development threatens to
evacuate the very category of the "political" as Schmitt defines
it: "The domination of 'capital' . . . can undermine an existing
political form and make it an empty façade . . . Should economic
thinking succeed in realizing its utopian goals and in bringing
about an absolutely unpolitical condition of human society, the
Church would remain the only agency of political thinking and
political form."[39] The Catholic Church is political for Schmitt for
interrelated reasons: it stands as a public, "visible institution," in
contrast to the "privatized" religion in the religiously tolerant
modern state produced by Weber's "inner-worldly" Protestant

37. Schwab, Introduction to *The Concept of the Political*, p. 4.
38. On Schmitt's dialogue with Weber, see G. L. Ulmen, Introduction to
*Roman Catholicism and Political Form*, pp. xiii-xxiv.
39. Schmitt, *Roman Catholicism and Political Form*, p. 25.

ethic,[40] and it derives its representational authority "from above," in contrast to modern parliamentary representation, which derives its authority from the people below.[41]

For Schmitt, the Catholic Church sustains the only authentic "power of representation" in the modern, capitalist world insofar as its representatives are simultaneously personal and transcendent. The Catholic Church "represents in every moment the historical connection to the incarnation and the crucifixion of Christ. It represents the Person of Christ Himself: God become man in historical reality."[42] The "representative figures" of the Catholic Church embody an ideal later transferred to the political sovereign at large in Schmitt's scheme: as authentic imitators of Christ, they mediate between God and man, the normal and the exceptional. They exemplify the *complexio oppositorum*, the "complex of opposites" that Schmitt identifies as the secret of the Church's powerful longevity: "there appears to be no antithesis it does not embrace."[43] Schmitt pushes beyond confessional boundaries, finding the *complexio oppositorum* to be a foundational dynamic characteristic of Christianity itself; it "holds sway over everything theological; the Old and New Testament alike are

40. Ibid., p. 32. George Schwab argues that Schmitt kept returning to the period of the seventeenth century precisely because of the close bond between the invention of the nation-state and the doctrines of religious tolerance produced as the painful solution to the wars of religion, a process initiated in the sixteenth century: "The Peace of Augsburg (1555), the religious compromise of Elizabeth I (1559-1563), and the Edict of Nantes (1598) were significant steps in the movement toward religious toleration—the recognition on the part of newly emerging sovereign rulers in distinct territorial states that Christians, regardless of specific doctrinal differences, were entitled to be treated as Christians and not as beings possessed by the devil to whom no quarter should be given." Schwab, Introduction to *Concept of the Political*, pp. 8-9.

41. Schmitt, *Roman Catholicism and Political Form*, pp. 25-26. Kahn comments on Schmitt's Catholic conception of representation, pp. 72-5.

42. Schmitt, *Roman Catholicism and Political Form*, p. 19.

43. Ibid., p. 7.

xl JENNIFER R. RUST AND JULIA LUPTON

scriptural canon; the Marcionitic either-or is answered with an as-well-as."[44] By generalizing the *complexio* as an essential trait of the "theological," Schmitt extends the possible frame of reference to any Christian regime. Both the sovereign and the Catholic representative figure personalize the divine; this personalization must, however, be distinguished from impersonation: in its modes of representation, the Church makes visible "the *complexio* of life in all its contradictions . . . molded into a unity of personal representation"[45]

Schmitt echoes this emphasis on the "unity of personal representation" in his much later work on *Hamlet*; Shakespeare's *Hamlet* may or may not be Catholic in its particular details, but it is at least partially "Catholic" in its mode of political representation. Hamlet engages Schmitt insofar as he perceives the character as a palimpsest of fictional and personal authority. Hamlet is a representation of religious schism by virtue of the fact that Shakespeare personalizes this schism by incorporating a sovereign figure who suffers from it. The exceptionality of *Hamlet*'s representation of sovereignty is evident in the claim that it is because this split itself is inherent in James I's troubled genealogy that it "intrudes" into the play of representation, contributing to the sense of irresolvable problem that has haunted analyses of *Hamlet*.

In a long footnote near the end of the second chapter of *Hamlet or Hecuba*, Schmitt reinforces the association between Hamlet, James and the irresolvable problems of religious schism by referring Hamlet's doubt about the theological status of the Ghost to differing views on ghosts current in post-Reformation England (p. 28, note 17). In this regard he anticipates more recent critics for whom the Ghost from "Purgatory" emblematizes the

44. Schmitt, *Roman Catholicism and Political Form*, p. 7. On Marcion, Schmitt, and political theology, see Jacob Taubes, *The Political Theology of Paul*, trans. Dana Hollander (Stanford: Stanford University Press, 2004).

45. Schmitt, *Roman Catholicism and Political Form*, p. 33.

Catholic element in the play, although Schmitt's opinion about Hamlet's attitude being precisely the "same" as James' Protestant views is not necessarily upheld by subsequent writers.[46] Apart from any associations with James, the Danish prince, home from Luther's Wittenberg in order to be accosted by a ghost from Purgatory, embodies the catastrophic split between Catholics and Protestants prior to the Peace of Westphalia insofar as he confronts the dilemma of reconciling conflicting claims to authority that may be glossed in confessional terms. The present corrupt court of Claudius may signify a Protestant emphasis on the radical immanence of a fallen world, at the same time that the Ghost may represent not simply the king murdered in the midst of this immanence, but also, through the metonym of Purgatory, Catholicism itself as a superseded system of ritual and belief, as it was by sovereign decree in Tudor and Stuart England.[47] While the Ghost may signify an echo or guilty memory of a pre-Reformation theological order, its appearance is too cryptic to allow this allegorical potential to emerge fully. Neither Catholic apologia nor anti-Papist polemic, the play's wilful obscurity about the theological status of its hero and setting is itself the drama's

46. See especially recent work by Stephen Greenblatt, *Hamlet in Purgatory* (Princeton: Princeton University Press, 2001) and *Will in the World* (New York: Norton, 2005). See also John Freeman "This Side of Purgatory: Ghostly Fathers and the Recusant Legacy in *Hamlet*," in *Shakespeare and the Culture of Christianity in Early Modern England*, ed. Dennis Taylor and David Beauregard (New York: Fordham University Press, 2003), pp. 222-259. On the tension in the play not only between Catholic and Protestant affiliations, but also between Calvinist and Lutheran strains of Protestantism, see Jennifer Rust, "Wittenberg and Melancholic Allegory: The Reformation and Its Discontents in *Hamlet*," in *Shakespeare and the Culture of Christianity in Early Modern England*, pp. 260-86. On the Catholic question in Shakespeare, see Richard Dutton, Alison Findlay, and Richard Wilson, eds., *Theatre and Religion: Lancastrian Shakespeare* (Manchester: Manchester University Press, 2003).

47. See Greenblatt, *Hamlet in Purgatory* and Freeman, "This Side of Purgatory."

most profound symptom of religious schism. Even if a Hamlet-James imbues the play with the aura of personal authority, that authority is always conflictual, and the Ghost lurks as a counterforce to this personalization, the specter of the ever-possible dissolution of the sovereign, as both political and spiritual force. The decay of "representation" is already well underway in *Hamlet*; the Ghost, we argue, is a *complexio oppositorum* that does not necessarily resolve into the "unity of personal representation."

In his reading of *Hamlet*, then, Schmitt moves from a kind of topical analysis (though conducted with great tact and sophistication) to something more modal, epochal, and structural concerning *Hamlet*. Something is rotten in the states of Europe because Christianity has fallen apart; the terrible *minus* of religious schism, however, leads to the extraordinary *plus* of the modern nation-state, the state whose monopoly on the political Schmitt sees besieged in the Weimar period. This is the political-theological calculus, devolving simultaneously on seventeenth- and twentieth-century stages, that makes Schmitt weep for the Renaissance. He weeps, that is, for the division of the Church, and he also laments the passing of the sovereign solution born out of that break.

Hamlet's world is pre-Westphalian, testing the overlapping borders of political and theological jurisdictions; our own world, according to Seyla Benhabib, is post-Westphalian, distinguished by an ever greater and more explosive mix of religious groups, more permeable national borders, and the rise of international and transnational forces and organizations.[48] As we have noted, the issue of Shakespeare and Catholicism has re-entered Shakespeare studies of late; reapproaching the question via Schmitt invites us to consider the problem at the political-theological level, and not only on the contextual or historicist plane. That is, what

---

48. Seyla Benhabib, *The Rights of Others: Aliens, Residents, and Citizens* (Cambridge, UK: Cambridge University Press, 2004), pp. 40-43.

kinds of sacral metaphors and exegetical rhythms constitute and conceptualize social and political groupings in Shakespearean drama? Moreover, how do these forms and figures regulate, or fail to regulate, divisions within Christianity as well as relations between Christians and non-Christians, in the pluralist world of Shakespeare's plays and in our own world? Such questions are not posed by Schmitt—indeed, he would be horrified but not surprised by the developments in liberalism they represent—but they are nonetheless enabled by the inevitable intrusion of time into the economy of Schmitt's own arguments. That these questions constellate much current research in Renaissance studies—from Stephen Greenblatt's *Hamlet in Purgatory* to forthcoming work by Victoria Kahn on Leo Strauss and Machiavelli—indicates both the relevance of political theology to the Renaissance and the relevance of the Renaissance to later political theology.

### 5. *Hamlet, Nomos,* and rogue thinking

In several places in *Hamlet or Hecuba,* Schmitt refers readers to a note in his major post-war work, *The* Nomos *of the Earth,* written several years earlier and definitively linked by Carlo Galli to the conceptual universe of Schmitt's Shakespeare reading (p. 26, note 15; and p. 66, note 50).[49] The footnote occurs in a section of *Nomos* that deals with the path to neutralizing the religious conflicts that tore apart the religious unity of medieval Europe in the sixteenth and seventeenth centuries. This neutralization involved re-imagining the early modern sovereigns of Europe as *magni homines* (great men) who fought wars with each other on the basis of their equal status; in this way, international conflicts came to be structured in the "form" of the "duel between

---

49. For a concise overview of *The* Nomos *of the Earth,* see Fredric Jameson, 'Notes on the *Nomos,*" *South Atlantic Quarterly* 104, no. 2 (Spring 2005): pp. 199-204. On *The* Nomos *of the Earth* and *Hamlet or Hecuba,* see Galli, "Presentazaione," pp. 14-17.

equals."[50] This formalization of aggression represented a transitional phase on the road to the modern European state. It was necessary to conceptualize the "power complexes" of Europe as "persons" in order to achieve an allegorical equivalence between the "war" and the "duel." This transitional stage required an element of human "fantasy." Schmitt delineates the contours of this "fantasy" in a passage that is crucial for grasping the conceptual subtext of his subsequent analysis of *Hamlet*:

> In human fantasy, they actually were sovereign persons, because they were the representative sovereigns of human persons, of the agents of old and newly crowned heads, of kings and princes not precisely specified. These kings and princes now could be "great men," because they had become absolute. They separated themselves from church, feudal, estate, and all other medieval ties, thereby entering into ties of a new spatial order.[51]

Schmitt's analysis of the role of "personification in the rise of the modern state" in *Nomos* echoes his elaboration of Benjamin's account of allegory in *Hamlet or Hecuba*. Schmitt notes that the "connection between representative persons" and "spatial power complexes" was indeed indebted to the "allegorical tendency of the Renaissance."[52] The allegorical impulse so thoroughly anatomized by Benjamin's book comes to represent for Schmitt in both *The* Nomos *of the Earth* and *Hamlet oder Hecuba* a bridge between medieval and modern modes of political representation and organization, a pivotal moment in which a "fantasy" structure comes to reorganize political realities. Türk aptly grasps the public scene of this "fantasy" for Schmitt's Shakespeare: "Far from signifying the transparency of a shared space separate from

50. Schmitt, *The* Nomos *of the Earth*, p. 143.

51. Ibid., pp. 143-44.

52. Ibid., p. 144. In a footnote on this same page, Schmitt claims: "Shakespeare's dramas, to the extent that they are political, also are determined by the same principle of political personalizations."

the private, the public sphere is constituted by individual sensitivity formed by an existential relation to the common."[53] Schmitt derives from Benjamin's *Trauerspiel* book an account of allegory as a collectively shared perceptual structure particular to the Renaissance and Reformation which articulates the transition from a seemingly more concrete medieval Christian unity to a more abstract, symbolically mediated normative state sphere. From the perspective of *Nomos*, the Hamlet-James of *Hamlet or Hecuba* appears as a kind of *magnum homo*, a specific manifestation of a larger process of constructing a new theologico-political imaginary in early modern Europe.

The "allegorical tendency of the Renaissance" contributed to the development of "forms" of "personification" that helped to quell the religious violence of early modernity and led in the long run to the development of the European state. England itself, however, was not, in Schmitt's view, destined to partake fully in such a process of state formation, at least in the sense that it occurred on the continent. One of the major lines of argument in *Nomos* (and another prong in Schmitt's critique of Benjamin) is that England itself represented a crucial exception to the European land order that came to be defined in terms of the entity of the "state." Within the "close-knit family" of European sovereign persons, England inserted a rogue element as the nation that broke away from the legal and political determinations based on the land to provide the "decisive spatial perspective"— the vantage point of the "sea" on the incipient European political situation.[54] In turning decisively toward the sea as a new medium of sovereignty and commercial expansion, England foreshadows

---

53. Türk, p. 82.
54. Schmitt, *The* Nomos *of the Earth*, p. 145.

the "rootlessness" [*Entortung*] of modern technology that will culminate in the dislocation of the modern European state.[55]

Schmitt's account in *Hamlet or Hecuba* of England's barbarism makes new sense in the context of *Nomos of the Earth*. Although Schmitt provisionally accepts Benjamin's characterization of Shakespeare as Baroque, he insists, *contra* Benjamin, on the fundamental difference between the Continental Baroque, governed by both classical rules and the emergence of modern state forms, and the Elizabethan Renaissance, whose cruder reception of classical elements also occurred within a distinct geopolitical orientation defined by the sea (with its lawless zones and pirate traditions as well as its fundamentally commercial outlook) rather than by land (with its more territorial and aristocratic traditions). It is no accident that Hamlet reenters Denmark from his aborted trip to England in Act Four with the help of *pirates*, types of an oceanic vagrancy in pursuit of permanent emergency, and hence also figures for England itself as a kind of rogue state with a special role to play in the reorganization of European and global spatial orders in both the early modern and the industrial periods.

This drive toward the sea, and ultimately, toward the regime of modern technology, has its own theological corollary: the "Puritan Revolution" of mid-seventeenth century England that dissolves the "decisionism of a juridical stamp" so characteristic of the continental European state.[56] This revolution also, of course, swept aside the Stuarts, James I's son Charles being its most celebrated victim. In the very last paragraph of his book on *Hamlet*, Schmitt reminds his readers of the unhappy fate of the Stuarts: "The Stuarts grasped neither the sovereign state of the European continent nor the transition to a maritime exis-

55. Ibid., p. 178. See also the penultimate paragraph in *Hamlet or Hecuba* (p. 67).
56. Schmitt, *The Nomos of the Earth*, p. 178.

tence that England achieved during their reign" (p. 67). The final view of the Stuart rulers articulated here is not quite nostalgic. Rather, Schmitt portrays James and his fellow Stuarts as perpetually anachronistic—a "hopeless" dead end rather than a missed opportunity. From this perspective, *Hamlet*'s mode of representation is not quite medieval, or "Catholic," and certainly not "baroque" in Benjamin's sense. In its odd distorting representation of an oddly distorted sovereign figure, the play is also potentially "revolutionary" insofar as Shakespeare, perhaps, comprehends, better than James himself could, that England is involved in a larger process of historical transformation, the "first phase" of "the century of English revolution" that would have profound global consequences (p. 67).

In the same soliloquy on Hecuba from which Schmitt takes the title of his essay, Hamlet calls himself a rogue: "O what a rogue and peasant slave am I." More than simply a sign of Hamlet's guilty consciousness, his cry also hits on a truth concerning Hamlet's own behaviour and capacities. He *is* a rogue, fully capable of the most gratuitous violence towards Polonius as well as Rosencrantz and Guildenstern. Like Schmitt's Elizabethan England, this perfect pattern of a prince also embodies elements that are "coarse and elementary, barbaric and not yet 'political'" (p. 41). What may appear at first glance to be a naïve or essentialist depiction of a simpler, more direct form of life must be read in relation to Schmitt's characterization of England's distinctive economic and political path in *The* Nomos *of the Earth*, a path that remained only partially integrated with respect to the rest of Europe and its own evolving institutions. The concrete immediacy that Schmitt discovers in Shakespeare's England can be understood as a *failure of mediation*—a situation in which certain kinds of structuring frameworks (such as that provided by the Catholic Church) have fallen away or become incapacitated, and in which the island's watery geography continually exposes the evolving English state to the lawlessness and opportunism of the sea.

Again, Adam Sitze, following Carlo Galli, is helpful here. In the modern state—the form of state that Schmitt associates with Continental Europe—the "mediation" provided by various representative organs, political ideas, and civil institutions such as the press attenuate and delay potentially bloody conflicts among factions and interests. The twentieth century underwent a *crisis in mediation,* such that the emergence of party politics and new liberal constitutions in Spain, Italy, and Germany—all instruments of mediation—led not to liberalization, but rather to the installation of Fascist governments and thus the "total" or "totalitarian" destruction of mediation as such. Sitze writes:

> Because the purpose of modern, rational political mediation was to keep the peace between the various factions that constitute any given political order, the result of this crisis is the impossibility of a reciprocal exclusion between politics and conflict. To the extent that this reciprocal exclusion is impossible—to the extent that politics and conflict become commensurable—the crisis in philosophical and political mediation becomes a crisis in modern politics in general.[57]

Sitze goes on to connect the at once raw and originary, subterranean and omnipresent, character of conflict in Schmitt's concept of the political to Schmitt's own piracy by and of history, his dangerous openness to the most "coarse" and "barbaric" elements in modern politics. Schmitt's depiction of Elizabethan England does not simply manifest what Schmitt elsewhere calls an "obscene romanticism" (p. 8), but also diagnoses the extent to which the conflictual core in politics reveals itself in *Hamlet* and in the world that *Hamlet* discloses as its own.

We might take Hamlet's murder of Polonius through the arras as an allegory of this disclosure and its multiple resonances across Schmitt's life, work, and times. Hamlet can only kill the

57. Sitze, p. 5.

king (or the man he takes for king) through the scrim formed by the tapestry hanging at the end of Gertrude's closet. The arras literally mediates—stands between—Hamlet and Polonius, providing Hamlet with just enough blindness so that he can slaughter the creature on the other side. Mediation fails not because it is nonexistent, but rather because it creates the conditions of a new and dangerous directness, allowing Hamlet to lunge at the man behind the curtain without looking him in the eye. Hamlet is, in Shakespeare's word, "rash." Gertrude exclaims, "O, what a rash and bloody deed is this!" to which Hamlet, discovering Polonius behind the curtain, responds, "Thou wretched, rash, and intruding fool, farewell" (3.4.26-31).[58] It is a bloody encounter between two rashnesses—that of the spying counsellor and the impulsive prince—and what permits their fatal collision is the fact of the screen.[59]

The arras in Gertrude's closet, like Schmitt's anti-theatrical reading of the play within the play, distinguishes not two separately configured spaces (one representational, the other belonging to the audience), but rather a continuous *real space*,

58. *Hamlet*, ed. Harold Jenkins (London: Methuen, 1982).

59. Although the thoughtful, melancholic Hamlet has dominated critical discourse, the idea of a rash and violent Hamlet has had its champions as well. The most prominent exponent of such a view within Shakespeare studies is G. Wilson Knight, who outlined the argument for a mean Hamlet in a series of essays; see for example "The Embassy of Death: An Essay on *Hamlet*," in *The Wheel of Fire* (New York: Routledge, 2001), pp. 17-49. A recent variation of this argument appears in Margreta de Grazia, *Hamlet without Hamlet* (Cambridge, UK: Cambridge University Press, 2007). At the opening of *Hamlet or Hecuba*, Schmitt refers to a Spanish variation on the same theme: "A world-renowned philosopher, Salvador de Madariaga, considers Shakespeare's Hamlet in a surprising new light in a 1948 book, *On Hamlet*. He makes him into an unscrupulous Renaissance man of action and violence, a Cesare Borgia" (p. 8). Madariaga (1886-1978) was a pacifist and an opponent of Franco; his *Hamlet* book argues that the Elizabethans were fully capable of being both "barbarous" and "supersubtle." Salvador de Madariaga, *On Hamlet* (London, Hollis & Carter, 1948), p. 34.

that is, a space in which real violence can occur. The failure of mediation describes not only Hamlet's rashness, but also Schmitt's own "rashness" with respect to the political conflicts of his time. Adam Sitze writes, "Prior to any occasionalism, it is this absence of philosophic mediation—this lack of any Idea in the Platonic sense—that permits Schmitt's opportunism, careerism, and racism to express itself with such virulence and enmity."[60] Schmitt perhaps most aptly becomes the Hamlet of his own essay not by virtue of the Prince's identifications with the philosopher-king James I, but rather because of Hamlet's uncanny, fundamentally unmediated condensation of a highly developed theoretical consciousness alongside a capacity for rash and violent thoughtlessness—the rogue character, that is, of their shared thought.

Schmitt's insight that the play space of *Hamlet* always remains open to the negative space of historical trauma thus does not simply apply to the family romance of the Stuarts in early modern England, but also, implicitly, to historical violence closer to Schmitt's own experience. When Schmitt speaks of the historical "taboo" that haunts *Hamlet,* he also calls to mind more recent taboos surrounding his own work in mid-twentieth century Germany—the taboo of the monstrous errors that led to his own and others' complicity in war and Holocaust. The veil of constitutionality allowed Schmitt to believe that Hindenburg, not Hitler, would be protected by the emergency clause.[61] An architect of the state of exception that legalized Hitler's rise to power, Schmitt also provided in *The* Nomos *of the Earth* an astute analysis of the way in which the modern doctrine of the just war provides the conceptual machinery for dehumanizing the enemy, and thus for mass killings on a scale unknown to ear-

60. Sitze, p. 7.

61. See Joseph Bendersky, *Carl Schmitt, Theorist for the Reich* (Princeton: Princeton University Press, 1983), for a nuanced, sometimes apologetic account of Schmitt's support of presidential powers, in order to shore up Hindenburg's presidency, during the period of Hitler's rise to power.

lier periods.[62] In the text of *Hamlet or Hecuba*, Schmitt indeed briefly links the "concrete reality" of the political context of *Hamlet* to concerns closer to his own era. In describing how the public sphere of Shakespeare's era seeps into the aesthetic structure of the play, Schmitt evokes an analogy to "a formula that has become quite common for topics with contemporary significance in the 1950s: *All characters and events in this production are fictional; any resemblance to real persons and events is purely coincidental*" (p. 35). Schmitt claims that Shakespeare, like the media producers of his own day, would have found such a warning label appropriate, since the "resemblances" that the formula dismisses as "coincidental" are symptomatic of real "political tension and agitation" (p. 35). In this passing analogy—as well as, perhaps, in Schmitt's text overall—the attempt to make the intrusion of history, of historical violence, into a taboo within the fictional work reveals the necessity to continue to probe the pressures of historical time within systems of representation and forms of life. Schmitt's life and work give us both an unparalleled case of these pressures, and some tools with which to begin understanding them. The taboo surrounding Schmitt's Nazism should not blind us to the potentialities of his thought, anymore than we should allow the instrumentality of his writing to sanitize or excuse its rogue character.

---

62. In *The Concept of the Political*, Schmitt argues that a war fought in the name of humanity "is necessarily unusually intense and inhuman because, by transcending the limits of the political framework, it simultaneously degrades the enemy into moral and other categories and is forced to make of him a monster that must not only be defeated but also utterly destroyed," p. 36. Schmitt elaborates the fundamental antagonism between the *justus hostis* of traditional international law (Roman and European) and the *justa causa* of twentieth century warfare in *The* Nomos *of the Earth*, pp. 320-22.

# HAMLET OR HECUBA:
## THE INTRUSION OF THE TIME INTO THE PLAY

Carl Schmitt

Why these Players here draw water from eyes:
For Hecuba! Why what is Hecuba to him, or he to Hecuba?
What would he do and if he had my losse?
His father murdred, and a Crowne bereft him.


—Hamlet 2.2, Text of the First Quarto [1603]

# Preface

The following pages discuss the taboo of a queen and the figure of the avenger. This discussion leads into the question of the true origins of the tragic action, the question of the source of the tragic, which I can only locate in a historical reality.

In this way I have attempted to comprehend *Hamlet* from out of its concrete situation. It will be helpful to the Shakespeare lover and the Shakespeare expert if I name here at the outset the three books to which I am indebted for valuable information and key insights: Lilian Winstanley, *Hamlet and the Scottish Succession* (Cambridge, UK: Cambridge University Press, 1921), German edition with the title *Hamlet, Sohn der Maria Stuart*, trans. A. Schmitt (Pfullingen/Württemberg: Verlag Günther Neske, 1952); John Dover Wilson, *What Happens in Hamlet* (Cambridge, UK: Cambridge University Press, 1935, 1951); Walter Benjamin, *Ursprung des deutschen Trauerspiels* (Berlin: Ernst Rowohlt Verlag, 1928).

Whoever has thought long enough about Shakespeare's *Hamlet* and its many interpretations is familiar with the unfathomable depths of this topic. He sees that many tracks lead into these depths but only a few lead out again. Whoever, in addition—like myself—arrives at the conclusion that Shakespeare's *Hamlet* has something to do with the historical King James, the son of Mary Stuart, runs into many taboos as well as the risk of additional misreadings. I could easily help my cause by citing the statement of a very well-known English author, who writes:

"About any one so great as Shakespeare, it is probable that we can never be right; and if we can never be right, it is better that we should from time to time change our way of being wrong."[1] This statement by T. S. Eliot offers us an inviting license, but I would like to use it only in the most extreme circumstances. Before that I would like to ask the reader for a few moments of his attention, presuming that the topic of *Hamlet* is dear to his heart. And this is something that I may be permitted to presume, as otherwise he would not have opened this book and read this preface.

1.  T. S. Eliot, "Shakespeare and the Stoicism of Seneca," *Selected Essays, 1917-1932* (Harcourt, Brace and Company, 1932). p. 107.

# INTRODUCTION

The drama *Hamlet, Prince of Denmark* has been the subject of an endless number of interpretations. The mournfully dressed, melancholy prince has become in the end a primal image of the human condition. The symbolic force of this figure has produced an authentic myth that finds its justification in a process of inexhaustible transformation. The eighteenth century poets of the German *Sturm und Drang*—Lessing, Herder, Goethe— began this process by making their own myth out of Hamlet. In Goethe's interpretation, Hamlet becomes a Werther who is destroyed by the burden of an all-too-heavy task. The nineteenth century made Hamlet into a passive anti-type of the active Faust and, at the same time, into a combination of genius and insanity. In the first third of our own twentieth century, the founder of the psychoanalytic school, Sigmund Freud, put forth the assertion that every neurotic is either an Oedipus or a Hamlet, depending on whether his neurosis is fixated on the father or the mother.

From such an excess of psychological interpretation, an inescapable labyrinth has been created. As Dostoyevsky himself, one of the greatest psychologists, has said, psychology is in fact a stick with two ends that one can turn around and around. As an understandable reaction against psychologism, a strictly historical approach originated after the First World War, primarily in Anglo-Saxon countries, that pointed to the indisputable contradictions and shortcomings in Shakespeare's plays, his dependence on literary predecessors, and his ties to the socio-economic order of his era. The traditional understanding of the strict unity of his characters and the artistic perfection of his works was destroyed. Shakespeare was now above all a dramatist of the Elizabethan age, his plays written for his London public. We will have more to say about this.

However, not even this historical objectification was able to put a stop to the endless stream of new interpretations of Hamlet. From different, and often even opposing, sides, Hamlet continues even today to function as a living myth. I take here two examples as signs of this inexhaustible mutability. A renowned German poet, Gerhart Hauptmann, published a play in 1935 with the title *Hamlet in Wittenberg*. It is not very strong. It remains trapped in psychologizing and contains painfully embarrassing digressions in which a subjectivist of the first half of the twentieth century seeks to foist his own erotic complexes onto Hamlet. But in spite of the sometimes obscene romanticism, a historical connection casts its shadow across this sad play. It is called "Hamlet in Wittenberg" without being equal to the powerful theme that is evoked by such a title. Nevertheless, it remains a strange indication that the Hamlet myth has not yet lost its power.

The other example comes from an entirely different direction, not from the north but from the south. A world-renowned philosopher, Salvador de Madariaga, considers Shakespeare's Hamlet in a surprising new light in a 1948 book, *On Hamlet*. He makes him into an unscrupulous Renaissance man of action and violence, a Cesare Borgia. The book is full of apt observations and uninhibited commentary; one can, however, imagine the kind of irony with which English critics have answered him, in which they could not refrain from noting that such an interpretation might be more easily explained by impressions from the Hitler years rather than from the Elizabethan age. Yet the secret of Hamlet demonstrates its unfathomability here once again in the startlingly new interpretation offered by a philosopher as significant as Madariaga, who unites in his spirit Spanish heritage with Anglo-Saxon education.

Interpretations and symbolizations of Hamlet are incidentally not limited to the psychology of the single human individual. Entire nations can also appear as Hamlet. Thus, in the nineteenth century, journalists of German liberalism like Börne and Gervinus recognized the tattered and fractured German people as a Hamlet, and a few years before the outbreak of the liberal revolution of 1848, Ferdinand Freiligrath wrote a poem, "Hamlet," that begins like this:

> Germany is Hamlet! Solemn and silent,
> Within his gates every night
> Buried freedom wanders,
> And beckons to the man on watch.

The comparison with the procrastinator and dreamer Hamlet who cannot take the decision to act is elaborately drawn with many details:

> He wove too many scholarly leavings
> His best deed is simply thought;
> He whiles too long in Wittenberg,
> In the lecture halls, or taverns.

In this way, the labyrinth becomes ever more impenetrable. I would now like to ask the reader to follow me for an hour into another region than that of psychological explanations, while still not remaining bound within the methods and results of the historical school. A nothing-but-historical perspective would be namely—after the dead end of psychologism—just another equally hopeless dead end, particularly if we remain stuck in nineteenth century philosophy of art. We must bear in mind the results of the psychological as well as those of the historical method, but we must not take them for the last word in *Hamlet* interpretation.

Instead, transcending both alternatives, the question of the source of the tragic action as such arises as a question that, if left unanswered, would render incomprehensible the entire specificity of the Hamlet problem. When one considers the extent to which the European spirit has demystified itself since the Renaissance, then it is in fact astonishing that such a strong and canonical myth as that of Hamlet could have emerged in Europe and from out of the essence of the European spirit. What caused a play of the last years of the Elizabethan age to produce that rare case of a modern European myth?

Let us turn our attention first to the dramatic events of the play itself, to the composition and structure of what one describes as the *hypothesis* in Greek drama, the *fable* of scholastic aesthetics, and what today one would call the *story*.[2] Let us stick close to the matter as it is presented in the play and ask: what is the action of the drama and who is the actor Hamlet, the hero of this drama?

2. The facts of the story, examined critically but with a will to understand, provide better insight than a polemical analysis or an apologetic concordance that seeks at all costs to maintain a specific aesthetic and a specific image of the poet. Laura Bohannan's article, "Miching Mallecho, That Means Witchcraft," *The London Magazine* (June 1954), is very informative in this regard as she conveys the experience of telling the story of *Hamlet* to a tribe of black Africans. The Africans asked some very reasonable questions that were for the most part more concrete and precise than the crude legal-historical material on the theme of revenge with which the famous jurist Josef Kohler confronts the reader in his otherwise very commendable book, *Shakespeare vor dem Forum der Jurisprudenz* (Würzburg: Stahel, 1883).

# The Taboo of the Queen

Hamlet is the son of a father who was murdered. The ghost of the murdered father appears and demands that the son avenge the murder. We thus have an ancient revenge theme and the typical opening situation for a revenge drama. But this opening also includes the fact that Hamlet's mother has married the murderer hardly two months after the murder with an unseemly and highly suspicious haste. In so doing, the mother has legitimated the murder and the murderer.

The first question that presents itself to every spectator and listener concerns the participation of the mother in the murder. Was she aware of the murder? Did she even perhaps instigate it? Did she abet it? Did she, before the murder, have a relationship with the murderer, without knowing anything about the murder itself? Or was she simply, like Queen Anne in *Richard III*, the victim of her own feminine susceptibility, and was she won over by the murderer only after the murder?

The question of the guilt of the mother poses itself right at the beginning of the drama and cannot be dismissed throughout the entire subsequent course of events. What should a son do if he wants to avenge his murdered father but in the process comes up against his own mother, now the wife of the murderer? The opening situation contains, as noted, an ancient theme of myth, legend, and tragedy. The equally ancient answer allows for only two possibilities. A son who is caught in this way in a conflict between the duty of vengeance and the bond to the mother has,

11

practically speaking, only two routes open to him. The first route is that of Orestes in Greek legend and the tragedy of Aeschylus: the son kills the murderer as well as his own mother. The other route is followed by the Amleth of the Nordic legend that Shakespeare knew and used: the son allies himself with his mother, and together they kill the murderer.

These are the two simple answers from Greek tragedy and Nordic legend. Even today, one would have to say that there is no third way and the mother cannot remain neutral, provided that one takes seriously the son's commitment to revenge and fully accepts the mother as a human person. The strangeness and opaqueness of Shakespeare's *Hamlet* is that the hero of the revenge drama takes neither one route nor the other. He neither kills his mother nor allies himself with her. Throughout the entire play, it remains unclear whether the mother was complicit in the murder or not. And yet, it would be important, even decisive, for the course of the plot as well as for the motives and deliberations of the avenger that the question of the guilt of the mother be clarified. But precisely this question, which poses itself throughout the entire play from beginning to end and ultimately cannot be suppressed, is carefully avoided throughout the drama and remains unanswered.

The question of the mother's guilt raises several further questions aside from her complicity in the murder. A particular topic of debate has been the extent to which, before the murder of her first husband, the mother was involved with the murderer. Hamlet speaks of the "incestuous marriage" and appears to suggest that the queen already had engaged in adultery with the murderer before the death of her first husband. J. Dover Wilson's book *What Happens in* Hamlet devotes an entire chapter to the question and comes to the conclusion that there can be no doubt that the adultery of the queen is a presupposition of Shakespeare's drama.[3] But not even that is indisputable.

In order to clarify this most important question of the mother's participation in the murder of the father, a range of *Hamlet* scholars have analyzed all the hints and clues in the play. Each word and gesture has been put under the magnifying glass, especially the play-within-the-play, which is of course designed to unmask the criminal. There are interpreters of Hamlet who believe that the mother is the real murderer. In the play-within-the-play (3.2.183-84),[4] the queen says: "A second time I kill my husband dead,/ when second husband kisses me in bed." In the nighttime confrontation between Hamlet and his mother in the queen's closet (3.4.27-30), when Hamlet believes that he has killed the king and sees that it was Polonius that he stabbed behind the arras, the mother cries: "Oh what a rash and bloody deed is this!" and Hamlet answers: "A bloody deed—almost as bad, good mother, as kill a king and marry with his brother." The queen repeats, horrified: "As kill a king!" Hamlet confirms, "Ay, lady, it was my word." One can take this remarkable dialogue, in particular, the words "kill a king," to mean that Hamlet really wanted to kill King Claudius instead of Polonius. But the line also allows itself to be interpreted as Hamlet intending to say that his mother has killed King Hamlet and married the murderer.

This interpretation, according to which the queen is actually the real murderer, has been advocated in particular with great zeal by my friend, Albrecht Erich Günther, who passed away in 1942. The legal philosopher and historian Josef Kohler, in his book, *Shakespeare vor dem Forum der Jurisprudenz*, decisively

3. John Dover Wilson, *What Happens in* Hamlet (Cambridge, UK: Cambridge University Press, First Edition, 1935; Second Edition, 1937), p. 39 ("Gertrude's Sin"), p. 292 ("The Adultery of Gertrude").

4. [Trans.: This and all other citations from *Hamlet* refer to William Shakespeare, *Hamlet*, ed. John Dover Wilson (Cambridge, UK: Cambridge University Press, 1934), unless otherwise noted.]

affirms that the mother shares in the guilt for the murder. Others deny any guilt or shared guilt for the murder on the part of the mother. For the audience member who follows the play and has no time to engage in psychological, philological, and legal-historical investigations, this decisive point remains clouded in darkness, and all the research has only confirmed the darkness, if not increased it. Every dramaturge or director who stages the play, however, must somehow deal with it. He has the possibility of suggesting to his audience different and even opposing answers. For what Hamlet does in the drama is entirely different, depending on whether guilt or innocence is attributed to the mother. Yet, in three hundred years one has not been able to reach a consensus on the guilt or innocence of the mother. And there will be no consensus, because there prevails in this matter an admittedly odd, but obviously deliberate and intentional obscurity.

We have three different printed texts of Shakespeare's *Hamlet*: the Quarto of 1603, a Quarto of 1604-1605 and the Folio of 1623.[5] In the 1603 Quarto, one finds a scene (4.6), from which one could conclude that the mother was privy to the revenge plan and was allied with her son against her second husband. This is missing in the later printings. In any case, the revenge of the son begins with an oddly restricted assignment. The ghost of the murdered father describes the murder and the murderer in the most gruesome way—Madariaga considers the all-too-gruesome description to be exaggerated and sensationalistic—he beseeches his son to avenge the outrageous murder, but then adds completely without commentary the additional restriction that the mother must be spared: "Nor let thine soul contrive against thine mother aught" (1.5.85-6). The mother should be left exclusively to her own conscience. Strange revenge drama! When Hamlet

---

5.  We can leave aside here the German text of *Der bestrafte Brudermord* [*Fratricide Punished*], which Dover Wilson designates as a fourth text (p. 56).

later reproaches his mother too pointedly in the queen's closet (3.4), the Ghost suddenly appears again, insists once more on the need for vengeance, and at the same time still urges leniency toward the mother. Thus, the mother is carefully kept out of the revenge assignment—that is to say, out of the dramatic core of the play.

We leave aside here all explanations that refer to patriarchy or matriarchy using a legal-historical approach or to father and mother complexes using a psychoanalytic perspective. Such explanations use the play only to illustrate general theories. Whoever attends without preconceived notions to the real experience of the play in its concrete form and its actual text soon recognizes that something is here enshrouded and evaded, whether it be out of concern for factual considerations or out of tact or due to some inhibition. In other words, we are confronted with a *taboo*, which the author of the play simply respects and which compels him to exclude the question of the guilt or innocence of the mother, even though it belongs morally and dramatically to the core of the revenge play. Even in the celebrated play-within-in-the-play (3.2), which is meant to exactly portray the murder and hold it up to the eyes of the murderer, she is excluded from involvement in the murder—at least in the existing text—in a conspicuous and, in the final analysis, also unnatural way.

One would not be able to say that the author of *Hamlet* avoided the awkward point out of delicacy and a generally sympathetic feeling for women. Shakespeare is otherwise very direct and open to the point of brutality in these things. He pursues no cult of the Lady and is not afraid to be straightforward when it comes to the guilt or innocence of women. His women are not Weimar ladies like Goethe's Princess Leonore or Iphigenia, nor are they Schillerian Theklas or Berthas. One need only think of the women in *Richard III* or *King Lear* or also of Ophelia in *Hamlet* itself. Hamlet's mother is by no means spared in the sense that she is delicately left in peace as a sensitive creature. Hamlet really speaks daggers to her, as he explicitly says himself (3.2.399).

Why then specifically in the case of Hamlet's mother is the question of guilt—essential though it is with regard to the murder and the taking of revenge—carefully avoided? Why is her complete *innocence* not at least clarified? If the poet were not bound to certain facts but really was free in his invention, then, in that case, he need only to show how things stand. Precisely this circumstance, namely that he clearly expresses neither guilt nor innocence, proves that a concretely determined inhibition and concern prevails here, a genuine taboo. The tragedy thereby takes on a peculiar character, and the revenge plot that constitutes the objective action of the play loses the simple clarity that it has in both Greek tragedy and Nordic legend.

I can name this very concrete taboo. It concerns Mary, Queen of Scots. Her husband, Henry Lord Darnley, the father of James, was brutally murdered in February 1566 by the Earl of Bothwell. In May of the same year, 1566, Mary Stuart married this very Earl of Bothwell, the murderer of her husband. This was hardly three months after the murder. Here one really can speak of an unseemly and suspicious haste. The question of the extent to which Mary Stuart was involved in the murder of her husband, perhaps even to the point of having instigated it herself, has remained unresolved and disputed to the present day. Mary maintained her complete innocence and her friends, especially the Catholic ones, believed her. Her enemies, above all Protestant Scotland and England, and all devotees of Queen Elizabeth, were convinced that Mary was in fact the real instigator of the murder. In Scotland, as in England, the whole affair was an outrageous scandal. But how was it a taboo at the time for the author of *Hamlet*? By then, the outrageous scandal had been publicly debated by both sides with fanatical zeal for decades.

The taboo can be explained precisely by the time and place of the origin and initial performance of Shakespeare's play, during the years 1600-1603 in London. This was the time in which all were expecting the death of the old Queen Elizabeth, and her successor was as yet undetermined. For all of England, these were years of the utmost tension and uncertainty. In addition to the general unrest of the era—civil and state wars between Catholics and Protestants all over Europe, religious and political persecutions of all kind—England faced in these years, the additional, barely tolerable tension that arose from the problem of the royal succession. The old Queen Elizabeth had reigned for forty years. In her hand lay a formidable political power. But she had no heirs and also delayed in naming a successor. No one risked discussing the sensitive issue in public. One Englishman who had spoken of it had his hand cut off as punishment. The queen refused to hear the "bells tolling" for her. But of course everyone talked about it in private, and the different groups and parties prepared for different successors. Some laid bets on a French prince, others on a Spaniard, others on a relative, Arabella Stuart. Even the execution of the famous sea-farer Sir Walter Raleigh in 1618 was partly influenced by his championing of Arabella Stuart over James.

Shakespeare and his troupe enjoyed the patronage of the Earls of Southampton and Essex. This group pinned their hopes on James, the son of Mary Stuart, as the future heir apparent. The group was at the time politically persecuted and oppressed by Elizabeth. The Earl of Southampton, a Catholic, was sentenced to death but not executed. The Earl of Essex, a former favorite and perhaps even lover, was executed by order of the old queen on February 25, 1601. His property was seized; Shakespeare's theater troupe had to leave London and play in the countryside, events that are directly alluded to in the opening of the players' scene, Act Two, Scene Two, of *Hamlet*. Elizabeth died on March 23, 1603.

Immediately after his accession to the throne in 1603, James pardoned the Earl of Southampton and returned to the Earl of Essex's widow the property confiscated upon her husband's execution by Elizabeth. Shakespeare's troupe was permitted to perform again in London and before the court. Shakespeare, along with other players, was appointed royal valet; he carried the title *King's Man* and wore the badge of the Lord Chamberlain.

Thus, in these critical years 1600-1603, all the hopes of the group to which Shakespeare's theatrical enterprise belonged were focused on James, son of Mary Stuart. In 1603, James actually succeeded Elizabeth to the throne of England, becoming the direct successor to the same queen who barely sixteen years before had ordered his mother's execution. James had always behaved very prudently vis-à-vis Queen Elizabeth in order not to endanger his own succession. But he nevertheless did not somehow disown his mother Mary Stuart. He venerated her memory and did not allow anyone to suspect or abuse her. In his book *Basilikon Doron* (1599), he admonishes his son in a solemn and moving manner to always hold the memory of this queen in honor.

These circumstances established the taboo of which we speak for the author of the tragedy *Hamlet*. Out of consideration for James, the son of Mary Stuart, the expected successor to the throne, it was impossible to insinuate the *guilt* of the mother in the murder of the father. On the other hand, the audience for *Hamlet*, as well as all of Protestant England and particularly of course London, was convinced of Mary Stuart's guilt. Out of consideration for this English audience, it was absolutely impossible to insinuate the *innocence* of the mother. Thus the question of guilt had to be carefully avoided. The plot of the drama became unclear and inhibited as a result. A terrible historical reality shimmers through the masks and costumes of the stage play, a reality which remains untouched by any philological, philosophical, or aesthetic interpretation, however subtle it might be.

## THE FIGURE OF THE AVENGER

The taboo of the queen is a powerful intrusion [*Einbruch*] of historical reality into Shakespeare's *Hamlet*. Next to this taboo stands a second, still more powerful intrusion: the transformation of the figure of the avenger into a reflective, self-conscious melancholic. The hero of the revenge play, the avenger himself, was problematized so thoroughly, in fact, that so far no one has been able to make a definitive determination concerning his character and behavior. Nowhere does Shakespeare provide an explanation for Hamlet's strange inactivity.[6] The result has been innumerable contradictions in the character of the hero and innumerable interpretations and constructions but not a single, clear answer.

We presume that Hamlet is for us in the first place just a stage figure, a mask, and not a historical hero. But precisely those Shakespeare scholars who remain consciously committed to the idea that we are dealing with nothing other than play come to the conclusion that Hamlet's character does not remain in suspension by chance. Robert Bridges writes: "Why has there been such question whether Hamlet was mad or only feigning, unless it was Shakespeare's design to make and leave it doubtful?"[7] The great lyric poet Keats thought that Shakespeare had left the question open "instinctively." John Dover Wilson, who refers to

6. Dover Wilson, [*What Happens in* Hamlet] p. 204: "Shakespeare, as everyone knows, never furnishes an explanation for Hamlet's inaction."

7. [Trans.: Bridges' question is cited by Dover Wilson, p. 220.]

both Bridges and Keats and discusses the question under the significant heading "Hamlet's Make-up," concludes that, whether intentional or instinctive, the result is this situation of suspension, which makes up part of the genius of the play.[8] In his celebrated essay on *Hamlet*, T.S. Eliot writes that *Hamlet* is "full of some stuff that the writer could not drag to light, contemplate, or manipulate into art."[9]

Whether the poet here *could* not bring something to light or whether, intentionally or instinctively, due to whatever consideration, he did not *want* to, is a question of its own. It remains indisputable that for some reason something is left open here. The three previously mentioned Shakespeare authorities, T.S. Eliot, Robert Bridges, and J. Dover Wilson, pay too much attention to the subjectivity of the poet and too little to the objective situation from which the drama emerges. Speculating on the subjectivity of the author can lead us no closer to a conclusion than the innumerable constructions of the madness or character of Hamlet have. The situation becomes clear when one takes into account the existing text and content of the play as well as the concrete situation in which it was written. Then it appears that—like the guilt of the queen—a piece of historical reality projects into the drama and helps to determine the figure of Hamlet as a contemporary historical figure that, for Shakespeare, his patrons, the actors, and the audience, was simply given and whose presence penetrates deep into the play. In other words, the stage character Hamlet is not completely subsumed by the mask. Intentionally or instinctively the conditions and forms of the original context within which the play was written have been brought into the

8. [Trans.: The conclusion to which Schmitt refers appears in Dover Wilson, p. 221.]

9. Cited in Dover Wilson, p. 305. [Trans.: The quotation is from Eliot's 1919 essay, "Hamlet and His Problems." Dover Wilson includes an appendix on "Mr. T. S. Eliot's Theory of *Hamlet*" toward the end of *What Happens in Hamlet* (pp. 305-308).]

play, and, behind the stage character Hamlet, another figure has remained standing. The spectators of that time also saw this figure when they saw Hamlet. Otherwise *Hamlet*, the longest and most difficult of Shakespeare's works, would not also have been simultaneously his most popular play. We too can recognize this other figure today if we are not blinded by the dogmas of a particular philosophy of art.

Shakespeare's *Hamlet* is structured as a revenge drama. The avenger, the hero of this revenge drama and thus the decisive figure, is rendered problematic by the poet himself in an incredible way. This odd avenger has justifiably not become famous as an avenger but, on the contrary, as a doubtful, problematic hero who has become uncertain of his revenge mission. Only through the problematization of the avenger did Shakespeare's play become what it is for us today, that is, something entirely different from a typical revenge drama. The revenge mission—along with the impulse to revenge—is distorted by the avenger's reflections, which do not simply relate to the practical means and methods of an unproblematic revenge, but turn this revenge itself into an ethical and dramatic problem. The hero of the revenge play, the avenger and perpetrator himself as form and dramatic figure, suffers an internal distortion of his character and motivation. We can call this the *Hamletization of the avenger.*

In two great soliloquies, this Hamlet spurs himself toward revenge by means of violent self-reproaches. The Ghost of the murdered father appears to Hamlet a second time "to whet thy almost blunted purpose" (3.4.111). In the entire first half of the play, up to the middle of Act Three, this peculiar avenger does nothing to carry out his revenge task other than organizing a play as a "Mousetrap" in order to convince himself that the Ghost of his murdered father is not a devil from hell (2.2.602-3).[10] The

---

10. I deal separately with the justifiably famous play-within-the-play below in the chapter on the "Source of the Tragic."

Amleth of Nordic legend that Shakespeare had used does not need a ghostly apparition to urge him to revenge. This Nordic Amleth does not doubt himself for a moment. Admittedly, like Shakespeare's Hamlet, he plays at madness, but in strong contrast to Hamlet, not as a doubter, but rather as a purposeful, practical man of action. The Amleth of Nordic legend is a born avenger, truly fanatic in his drive to revenge. It is in fact, as Lilian Winstanley aptly puts it, something of a paradox that precisely the hero of a revenge play should become a Hamlet in the modern sense, broken and inhibited by reflections. The astonishing transformation of the typical avenger, the deformation and refraction in the character of the hero of a revenge drama, this entirely surprising turn toward weakness caused by reflection, only becomes comprehensible in the context of the historical situation of 1600-03, and through the central figure of these years, King James.

I do not claim that Shakespeare's Hamlet might be a copy of King James. Such a copy would not only be inartistic, it would also have been politically impossible. From the point of view of the history of the era, one finds in *Hamlet*, just as in other Shakespearean plays, the many historical and political implications often discussed by Shakespearean scholars. However, for an insightful interpretation of *Hamlet* it becomes necessary to distinguish several degrees and kinds of historical influences. Otherwise, the danger arises that the countless ephemeral references will be placed on the same level with essential receptions. Without a doubt, there are thousands of allusions and innuendos in Shakespeare's work, of which many are hardly understood today and also need not be understood. They are occasional and incidental references to contemporary historical events and persons, accommodations and considerations that contemporaries would have immediately understood, but were already no longer noticed a few years later.

Out of the endless multitude of these cases, I note three examples of mere *allusions* in *Hamlet*, one well-known and two less-well-known, in order to demonstrate what is meant here. Act Four of *Hamlet* (4.4.18ff) alludes, in a way comprehensible only to the English audience of that time, to the sand dunes of the Ostende that the English had heroically defended against the Spanish in 1601.[11] Less well-known is the allusion to the coronation of King James I in July 1603 in Act One of *Hamlet* in Laertes' speech, in which he justifies his voyage from France to the court of King Claudius by referring to his coronation (1.2.54). This coronation is first mentioned in the Second Quarto [1604-05] and is not found in the First Quarto [1603], which establishes the actual reference to the coronation of July 1603.[12] Conversely, in the third example a passage is suppressed for contemporary historical reasons. In his soliloquy "To be or not to be" (3.1.56ff), Hamlet enumerates a series of grounds for suicide; *a tirants raigne,* a tyrannical regime, is found in the First Quarto as a motive for fleeing life. This phrase is missing from the Second Quarto because James was sharply sensitive about this point.

Such allusions have something incidental about them; today they are for the most part only significant from a literary-historical perspective. A second kind of historical influence, which one can describe as true *mirrorings* [*Spiegelungen*], is quite different. Here, a contemporary event or figure appears in the drama as in a mirror and determines a picture there in its lines and colors. For our topic, an important example is the influence of the character and fate of the Earl of Essex. It has often been noted, since Malone, that Horatio's parting words on the death of Hamlet (5.2.357-8) are the parting words that Essex had spoken to his

---

11. [Trans.: Schmitt seems to refer to the following lines: "Truly to speak, and with no addition,/ We go to gain a little patch of ground/ That hath no profit in it but the name" (4.4.18-20).]

12. [Trans.: At this moment, Laertes asks for Claudius' "leave and favor to return to France,/ From whence . . . willingly I came to Denmark/ To show my duty in your coronation" (1.2.53-55).]

executioner on the scaffold.[13] An expert like John Dover Wilson, in his *Essential Shakespeare*, even defends the idea that the Earl of Essex, with his melancholy and some of his other features, was the model for Hamlet, if there ever was one.[14] In his edition of *Hamlet*, Dover Wilson also has included, in lieu of any other picture, a portrait of the Earl of Essex in the year 1594.

It appears to me that the doubtlessly strong influence that the figure and fate of the Earl of Essex exerts on the play principally affects the second half of the drama, after the exposure of the murderer. This second part is less a revenge drama than a life and death struggle between Hamlet and King Claudius. That King James could offer no model for the death of Hamlet goes without saying. But the details of Essex's imprisonment and execution were all the more present, and the group to which Shakespeare belonged was deeply shocked by them. Thus, features of the character and fate of the Earl of Essex wove themselves into the image otherwise determined by James. This is not unnatural because such stage plays form a kind of "dream-frame" [*Traumrahmen*], as Egon Vietta has noted. Just as people and realities merge with each other in a dream, images and figures, events and situations are interwoven in a dream-like way on stage. At the end of the play, however, an allusion of the first degree again appears, not a mirroring but an innuendo. The dying Hamlet names Fortinbras as his successor and gives him his voice, his *dying voice* (5.2.354).

---

13. [Trans.: The lines from *Hamlet* to which Schmitt refers are "Good night, sweet prince/ And flights of angels sing thee to thy rest." The chapter on "Essex and Hamlet" in Lilian Winstanley's book, *Hamlet and the Scottish Succession* (London: Cambridge University Press, 1921), cites Malone's observation. Essex's last words on the scaffold were reportedly: "'And when my soul and body shall part, *send thy blessed angels to be near unto me which may convey it to the joys of heaven*'" (quoted in Winstanley, p. 144)].

14. [Trans.: J. Dover Wilson discusses Essex as the model for Hamlet in *The Essential Shakespeare: A Biographical Adventure* (Cambridge, UK: Cambridge University Press, 1932), p. 103-107, where he concludes: "Hamlet's mystery is the mystery of Essex" (p. 106).]

This has an obviously political implication that functions as an acclamation *before* the accession of James to the throne in 1603 and as an act of homage to James *after* the accession, and was also understood as such.

Next to the fleeting allusions and the true mirrorings, there is yet a third, highest kind of influence from the historical present. These are the structurally determining, genuine *intrusions* [*Einbrüche*]. They cannot be common and ordinary, but their consequences are that much stronger and deeper. The involvement of Mary Stuart in the murder of James' father and the transformation of the figure of the avenger in view of King James belong to this category, which bestows on the actual revenge drama the special character that we associate with the name of Hamlet today.

Despite the intense mirroring of the life and death of the Earl of Essex that penetrates into the drama, it is not the case that there would now be, as it were, two Hamlets, the James-Hamlet of the first part and the Essex-Hamlet of the second part. We see here rather the superiority of the genuine intrusion over the simple—even if authentic—mirroring. The play *Hamlet* on the whole retains its arrangement as a revenge play; the murder of the father and the marriage of the mother to the murderer remain its foundation. Consequently, James-Hamlet remains the key figure, and the problematic of the figure of the avenger stems from the contemporary historical presence of Mary Stuart's son. The philosophizing and theologizing King James embodied namely the entire conflict of his age, a century of divided belief and religious civil war. The distortion that differentiates the Hamlet of this drama from all other avenger figures and that is otherwise inexplicable, even through reference to the fate and character of the Earl of Essex—in short, the Hamletization of the avenger—

finds a suitable explanation only here, in James. It is here that the connection between present history and tragedy emerges. [15]

15. F. G. Fleay especially has studied the references to current events in Shakespeare's plays. [Trans.: Schmitt appears to be referring to Fleay's *A Chronicle History of the Life and Work of William Shakespeare, Player, Poet, and Playmaker* (London: J. C. Nimmo, 1886).] With regard to James I, the forword to the German edition of Lilian Winstanley's book, *Hamlet, Sohn der Maria Stuart* (Pfullingen: Verlag Günther Neske, 1952) lists some older examples. [Trans: Winstanley's book was originally published in English as *Hamlet and the Scottish Succession* (London: Cambridge University Press, 1921).] In her book on *Hamlet*, in a chapter entitled "*Hamlet* and Essex," Winstanley offers numerous citations and references. In general, the connection with the fate of the Earl of Essex has long been known. I recall merely the fifty-fourth essay of Lessing's Hamburg dramaturgy and Richard Schiedermair's book, *Der Graf von Essex in der Literatur* (Kaiserslautern: Hermann Kayser, 1908-09).

A larger topic arises here: the political symbols and allegories in Shakespeare's drama. Lilian Winstanley devoted her life's work to this topic. In addition to her book on *Hamlet*, the following publications are primarily to be mentioned: *Macbeth, King Lear and Contemporary History, being a study of the relations of the play of James I, The Darnley Murder and the St. Bartholomew Massacre and also of King Lear as Symbolic Mythology* (Cambridge, UK: Cambridge Press, 1922) and *Othello as the Tragedy of Italy, showing that Shakespeare's Italian contemporaries interpreted the story of the Moor and the Lady of Venice as symbolizing the tragedy of their country in the grip of Spain* (London: T. Fisher Ltd., 1924). Moreover, she has written an unpublished manuscript on *The Tempest*. It is not a question of whether one can always follow Winstanley's interpretations or might consider much about them to be contrived and artificial. The underlying approach is perceptive and productive.

The intellectual historical problem has been treated by Walter Benjamin in "Allegory and *Trauerspiel*," *Ursprung des deutschen Trauerspiels* (1928), p. 155-236 [*The Origin of German Tragic Drama*, trans. John Osborne (London: New Left Books, 1977), p. 159-235]. The task would now be to link the theses and material from Winstanley with the thoughts of Benjamin and to go deeper into the problem of allegory. I can only allude to this task here. I would reserve it for myself, if, for personal reasons, I were not prevented from making further plans and proposing publications. A brief indication may be found in my book, *Der Nomos der Erde im Völkerrecht des Jus Publicum Europaeum* (Cologne: Greven-Verlag, 1950), p. 116-117 [*The Nomos of the Earth in the International Law of the Jus Publicaum Europaeum*, trans. G. L. Ulmen (New York: Telos Press Publishing, 2006), p. 144].

The unhappy Stuart lineage from which James descended was more deeply involved than others in the fate of the European schism of belief. James' father was murdered; his mother married the murderer; the mother for her part was executed; James' son, Charles I, likewise died on the scaffold; the grandson was deposed from the throne and died in exile. Two Stuarts thus died on the scaffold; only eight of seventeen rulers of the Stuart name reached the age of fifty.[16] James is one of these and one of the few Stuarts who died a natural death in possession of the crown. But his life was nevertheless disrupted and imperiled enough. As a child of one and a half years he was crowned king. All parties sought to take control of his person. He was robbed, kidnapped, arrested, jailed and threatened with death. Often as a boy and youth he remained awake and dressed throughout the night so that he could immediately flee. He was baptized as a Catholic, but was removed from his mother and reared as a Protestant by her enemies. His mother, Mary Stuart, died as a devotee to her Roman Catholic beliefs. The son, to avoid losing the throne of Scotland, had to ally himself with the Protestants. He had to put himself on good terms with his mother's enemy to the death, Queen Elizabeth, in order to win the throne of England. He was thus literally from the womb immersed in the schisms of his era. No wonder that he became cunning and duplicitous and learned

[Trans.: The number for footnote 15 is omitted in the main text of both German editions. We have chosen to place it at the end of the current paragraph because the focus of the note seems to correspond most closely to the ideas articulated in this part of the main text. However, the French translation, *Hamlet ou Hécube: L'irruption du temps dans le jeu*, trans. Jean-Louis Besson and Jean Jourdheuil (Paris: L'Arche, 1992), places the footnote number after the following assertion in an earlier paragraph: "This has an obviously political implication that functions as an acclamation *before* the accession of James to the throne in 1603 and as an act of homage to James *after* the accession, and was also understood as such" (p. 25).]

16. Eva Scott, *Die Stuarts*, trans. Elisabeth Mayer (Munich: Callwey, 1936), p. 20.

to deceive his enemies. Yet he also displayed moments of improbable courage as well as fits of sudden violence.

This unhappy son of an unfortunate lineage, who asserted himself painstakingly between his Catholic mother and her Protestant enemies, between intriguing courts and unruly noble factions, between fanatically disputing priests and preachers, was a great reader and writer of books, a friend of sharp-witted speech and ingenious formulations, a famous writer and debater in an age of theological controversy and dispute. In 1597, he wrote a *Daemonologie* in which he treats the problem of ghostly apparitions in the same way it is understood in Shakespeare's *Hamlet*. The point of departure for Hamlet's doubt and "inaction" is the paralyzing question of whether the ghost of his father that appears to him might be a devil from hell. This question only becomes meaningful and concrete in terms of the contrast between Catholic and Protestant demonologies of the time.[17] Above all, however, James defended the divine right of kings with great fervor in treatises and disputes. This also reappears in Shakespeare's plays, particularly in *Hamlet*.[18] Concerning the

---

17. Dover Wilson, *What Happens in* Hamlet, p. 62, gives an account of the three different views on ghosts and ghostly apparitions in a particularly informative analysis. At that time in England, there was a Catholic view according to which the apparition comes from Purgatory; a Protestant view according to which it mostly comes from hell as a treacherous devil; and an enlightened skeptical view, which is contained especially in a 1584 book by Reginald Scot [*Discoverie of Witchcraft*]. This book was later burned by executioners on the order of James. In Act One, Hamlet's doubt is based on the Protestant views for which James had also argued. The Ghost is according to this view real and not the mere hallucination of a melancholy mind. The connection between Hamlet and James becomes tangible here, at the crucial outset of the plot, and I do not understand why Dover Wilson does not mention it. Or might a taboo rule over this point as well?

18. A leading constitutional historian in the United States, Charles Howard McIlwain, has edited the *Political Works of James I* with an outstanding introduction as volume I of the Harvard Political Classics (Cambridge, MA: Harvard University Press, 1918). I owe thanks to Miss Lilian Winstanley in

divine right of kings James conducted a great—although also obviously futile—dispute with the famous Jesuits Cardinal Bellarmin and Francisco Suarez, the neo-Thomist systematic theologian, both of whom were more modern than James. The divine right of kings was his true life's task, his existential problem. For him, it was at root a sacred blood right and could only be claimed by kings who ascended to the throne through legitimate succession, not by usurpers. James' theories thus accorded with his existence; his being was tattered, but his consciousness was not just patched together.[19]

Yet his ideological position was simply hopeless. Catholics and Protestants, Jesuits, Calvinists, and Puritans, and above all, the dangerous philosophers of the Enlightenment finished him off, not just his theories but also his image. The propaganda of his political enemies made him into an unsympathetic, half-mad pedant, a ridiculous buffoon with rickety legs, goggle eyes, and a slobbering tongue.[20] He has found truly intelligent defenders, though, among them Isaak Disraeli, the father of the famous Benjamin Disraeli, who deserves mention because he points out the political caricature for what it was and maintains that if James had carried off a great victory, he would be as respected as a writer as Fredrick the Great. But the unfavorable image prevails

Aberysthwyth (Wales) for the unpublished manuscript of an essay on Shakespeare's *Tempest*, which contains important new material on the topic of the "divine right of kings" in Shakespeare.

19. In his philosophical notebook from the Jena era, Hegel writes: "A patched-up sock is better than a tattered one; not so for self-consciousness" *Dokumente zu Hegels Entwicklung*, ed. Johannes Hoffmeister (Stuttgart: Frommann, 1936), p. 370.

20. [Trans: Schmitt seems to derive many of these details from a description of James I cited by Dover Wilson in *The Essential Shakespeare*, chapter VI: "'his big head, his slobbering tongue, his quilted clothes, his ricketty legs, his goggle eyes . . . his gabble and rodomontade, his want of personal dignity, his vulgar buffoonery, his pedantry, his contemptible cowardice' disgusted all who had to do with him" (p. 114).]

to this day. Even in the recently (1952) published history of the English Revolution by the Kiel historian Michael Freund, James appears as a grotesque figure. Yet Michael Freund must also recognize that the unhappy Stuart, in spite of his impotent will, saw far more clearly than most of his contemporaries.

The warped image of this king severely hampers our perception of his connection with Shakespeare's Hamlet and scares the majority of Shakespeare scholars away.[21] Nevertheless, it remains clear that the distortion of the avenger figure can only be explained by the historical presence of King James. In times of religious schisms the world and world history lose their secure forms, and a human problematic becomes visible out of which no purely aesthetic consideration could create the hero of a revenge drama. Historical reality is stronger than every aesthetic, stronger also than the most ingenious subject. A king who in his fate and character was the product of the strife of his age itself stood before the eyes of the writer of the tragedy in his own existence. Shakespeare and his friends were at the time betting on James

21. This is evident also in chapter VI of Dover Wilson's *Essential Shakespeare*. Consequently the English Shakespeare scholar arrives at this thesis: "Apart from the play . . . there is no Hamlet" (p. XLV of the Introduction to his edition of *Hamlet*). This is exactly the question. In the next chapter on the source of the tragic, we will formally develop the opposing thesis by distinguishing play from tragedy and eliminating the prejudices of a romantic aesthetic that sought to make Shakespeare into a kind of ingenious, refined Schikaneder with a hint of Wordsworth and Keats. [Trans.: Schmitt refers here to Emanuel Schikaneder (1751-1812) a German dramatist who wrote the libretto for Mozart's *Magic Flute*. In *Roman Catholicism and Political Form* (1923), trans. G.L. Ulmen (Westport, CT: Greenwood Press, 1996), Schmitt attacks The Magic Flute as a "hymn of the Enlightenment." He focuses particularly on the "diabolical . . . contempt for the common man depicted in the character of Papageno." He concludes by drawing a negative contrast between Mozart's opera and Shakespeare's *Tempest*: "There is nothing more frightful than this beloved opera, if only one takes the time to understand it in the wider context of the history of ideas. One must compare it with Shakespeare's *Tempest* and recognize how Prospero has become a Masonic priest and Caliban a Papageno" (p. 34).]

as the coming heir to the throne; he was their hope and their dream in a desperate moment of crisis and catastrophe. John Dover Wilson is right when he says that with the execution of the Earl of Essex on February 25, 1601, the Elizabethan era came to an end, and, with it, Shakespeare's most proper and beautiful environment disappeared. James disappointed the hopes of the poets and actors. But hope and dream had by then found their way into the brilliant play. The figure of Hamlet had entered into the world and its history, and the myth began its journey.

# THE SOURCE OF THE TRAGIC

Once we recognize in the guilt of the queen and in the figure of the avenger two historical intrusions into the drama, we confront the last and most difficult question: Should historical arguments even be included in the consideration of a work of art? From where does the tragedy derive the tragic action upon which it lives? What is—in this general sense—the source of the tragic?

At this level of generality the question is almost discouraging. The difficulty presents itself at first as a technical problem. Owing to an extreme division of labor, academic fields and disciplines have become specialized. Literary historians work with different material and different perspectives than political historians. Shakespeare and his Hamlet belong to the realm of literary historians, while Mary Stuart and James I are the responsibility of political historians. Consequently, Hamlet and James encounter each other only with great difficulty. The rift is too deep. Literary historians consider the source of a drama to be a literary source, either a precursor or a book that Shakespeare used: for *Julius Caesar*, Plutarch; or for Hamlet, the Nordic saga of *Saxo Grammaticus* in its sixteenth century literary adaptations.

Another difficulty stems from a broadly prevailing philosophy of art and aesthetics. Its relation to the problem of the division of labor need not concern us here. In any case, philosophers of art and teachers of aesthetics tend to understand the work of art as an autonomous creation, self-contained and unrelated to historical or sociological reality—something to be understood only on its own terms. To relate a great work of art to the actual politics of the time in which it was created would presumably obscure its purely aesthetic beauty and debase the intrinsic worth of artistic form. The source of the tragic then lies in the free and sovereign creative power of the poet.

We thus confront sharp distinctions and fundamental divisions, boundaries and barriers between opposing approaches; complete value systems, which recognize only their own passports and certifications, validate only their own visas, allowing others neither entrance nor passage. We will attempt in our consideration of Shakespeare's *Hamlet* to avoid this dangerous fragmentation and find a better approach. In so doing, we must bear in mind that these difficulties are exacerbated by the entrenched views of our German cultural tradition.

## The Creative Freedom of the Writer

We have become accustomed in Germany to looking upon the writer as a genius who can create from whatever sources he chooses. The cult of genius that arose during the German *Sturm und Drang* period of the eighteenth century has become a *credo* of the German philosophy of art, precisely with respect to Shakespeare's supposed arbitrariness. The creative freedom of the writer becomes thereby a defense of artistic freedom in general and a stronghold of subjectivity. If his genius so compels him, why should an artist not be able to utilize artistically whatever he wishes and in whatever manner he wishes, be it personal experience or that of others, books or newspaper articles? He enters into and transports the stuff of life into the totally other realm of the beautiful, where historical and sociological questions become tactless and tasteless. The old poetics spoke of "poetic license," which in German becomes the "poetic freedom" that expresses the sovereignty of the poetic genius.

It is also significant that German aesthetic concepts are generally determined more by poetry than by drama. When discussing literature, we tend to think of a lyric poem more readily than a drama. The relation of a lyric poem to literary experience is something entirely different from the relation of tragedy to its mythical or historical sources. In this sense, the lyric poem has no source; it finds its occasion in a subjective experience. One of our greatest and most form-conscious writers, Stefan George, says: Experience undergoes such a transformation through art that it becomes meaningless for the artist himself, while for others knowledge of this experience is more bewildering than redemptive. That may be true for a lyric poem and may refute the pedants who attempt to garnish Goethe's love poems with his romantic experiences. But the freedom to create, which provides the lyric poet with such free play vis-à-vis reality, cannot be conferred upon other types and forms of literary creation. The subjectivity of the lyric poet corresponds to a type of creative freedom that is different from that which belongs to the objectivity of the epic writer and also different from that of the dramatist.

In Germany we have an image of the dramatist that, understandably, is drawn from the model of our great dramatic writers. Lessing, Goethe, Schiller, Grillparzer, and Hebbel all wrote their dramas as books for publication. They sat at their desks or stood at their writing tables as "domestic workers" and delivered polished manuscripts to a publisher for an honorarium. The term "domestic worker" (*Heimarbeiter*) is not used here disparagingly; it is merely the proper designation of a sociological state of affairs important for our problem and indispensable for our discussion, because Shakespeare's plays were produced in a completely different way. He wrote them not for posterity but for his concrete and immediate London public. Strictly speaking, one could say he did not write them. Rather he drafted them for a very specific audience. Not one of Shakespeare's plays anticipated spectators who had read it beforehand and recognized it from a published book.

All the above-mentioned German conceptions of art and the work of art, the drama and the dramatist, prevent an impartial view of Shakespeare and his work. Let us leave aside the debate about Shakespeare the person. One thing is certain: he was no "domestic worker" in the literary production of book-dramas. His plays originated in direct contact with the London court, the London public, and London actors. Intentional or unintentional references to contemporary events and persons arose quite naturally, whether as mere allusions or true mirrorings. In times of political tension and agitation such references were unavoidable. We recognize this in our own time and need only recall a formula that has become quite common for topics with contemporary significance in the 1950s: *All characters and events in this production are fictional; any resemblance to real persons and events is purely coincidental.* I certainly do not mean to treat the author of Hamlet on the same level with contemporary producers of films and period plays. But the analogy of references to current events is revealing, and Shakespeare would certainly not have been averse to prefacing his dramas with such a statement.

All this not only contributes to our understanding of the psychology and sociology of the playwright, but also to the concept of drama and our question concerning the source of tragic action. It is here that the limits of the invention of the writer become clear. An author of plays intended for immediate performance before a familiar audience not only enters into a psychological and sociological interaction with this audience but also shares with it a common public sphere. Through its concrete presence, the assembled audience establishes a public sphere that encompasses the author, the director, the actors, and the audience itself and incorporates them all. If the audience does not understand the action of the play, it simply does not remain engaged and the public sphere dissolves or ends in a mere theatrical scandal.

Such a public sphere places a strict limit on the creative freedom of the playwright. Observance of this limit is guaranteed by the fact that the audience will no longer follow the events on stage if they deviate too much from the audience's knowledge and expectations and become incomprehensible or meaningless. The knowledge of the audience is an essential factor of the theater. Even the dreams that the dramatist weaves into his play must be able to become the dreams of the spectators, with all the condensations and displacements of recent events. The creative freedom of the lyric poet is a separate issue, as is that of the epic writer and the novelist. But the subjectivity and the creative inspiration of the dramatist is severely restricted both by the knowledge of the spectators following the performance and by the public sphere established by the spectators' presence.[22]

One should not be fooled by the seemingly limitless freedom Shakespeare exercised with respect to his literary sources. He certainly took great liberties. One might even characterize him as "essentially anti-historical."[23] Yet his arbitrary use of literary sources is only the other side of a much firmer tie to his concrete London audience and its knowledge of contemporary reality. In historical dramas which presume a knowledge of past history, this audience knowledge is deployed differently than in dramas tied to current events. The historical drama references persons and events with names that are familiar to the audience and call up certain conceptions and expectations relevant to the author's purposes. Jean Paul's dictum holds true for such spec-

---

22. Richard Tüngel, an experienced journalist, has written: "One of the essentials of dramatic effect is that the spectators know and understand more about what is happening or will happen on the stage than the actors. One could say that allowing the audience to know more than the characters on the stage is one of the most effective techniques available to dramatic art. Shakespeare made use of it in many of his dramas and comedies. It is very possible that the historical presence of the Hamlet drama—its allusion to the Scottish tragedy—had such an effect upon the audience at that time." *Die Zeit* 45 (November 6, 1952).

23. See the essay on Paul Ernst, "The Metaphysics of Tragedy," in Georg Lukács, *Soul and Form* (Cambridge, MA: MIT Press, 1974).

tator historical knowledge: "When the writer summons him, a familiar historical character—for example, Socrates or Caesar—enters like a sovereign, preceded by his reputation. A name here is a myriad of situations." The effect is different, but no less forceful, when a person from contemporary history appears under a different name but is nonetheless immediately recognizable to the spectators. In this case, the transparent *incognito* heightens the tension and the participation of the knowing spectators and listeners. This was in fact the situation in the case of Hamlet-James that concerns us here.

## Play and Tragedy
Yet the knowledge of the spectators is not the only essential factor in the theater; it is not only the audience that pays attention to the observance of the rules of the game and of language. The theater itself is essentially play. The play is not only played out on stage, it is play in and of itself. Shakespeare's plays, in particular, are true theatrical plays: comic plays [*Lustspiel*] or tragic plays [*Trauerspiel*]. The play has its own sphere and creates a space for itself within which a certain freedom is maintained both from the literary material as well as from the originating situation. Thus it creates its own field of play in both space and time. This makes possible the fiction of a completely self-contained, internally self-sufficient process. Thus Shakespeare's plays can be performed as pure play, without reference to any historical, philosophical, or allegorical connotations or other extraneous considerations. This is true also for *Hamlet*, wherein most of the action and most of the scenes are pure play. Otto Ludwig already noted and justifiably emphasized this in his *Dramatische Studien*.[24]

24. Otto Ludwig repeatedly emphasizes that a drama must be heard and understood in terms of its "inner relationships," i.e., from within the drama itself. He is thus unrelenting in his criticism of Hegel, who was presumably too much of a sociologist to be satisfied with attending just to the internal development of a play in and of itself. Full of irritation, Ludwig cites what

I do not expect anyone to think of James I when Hamlet is on stage. I would also not want to measure Shakespeare's Hamlet against the historical James I or vice-versa. It would be absurd, after viewing a well-played performance of *Hamlet*, to be distracted from the play by historical reminiscences. Nevertheless, we must distinguish between *Trauerspiel* and tragedy.[25] Unfortunately, we Germans have become accustomed to translating the word "tragedy" with *Trauerspiel*, thus blurring the distinction. Shakespeare's dramas, which end with the death of the hero, are called "tragedies"; likewise, the play *Hamlet* is called a "tragical history" or a "tragedy."

Yet it is still necessary to distinguish between *Trauerspiel* and tragedy to separate them so that the specific quality of the tragic is not lost and the seriousness of a genuine tragedy does not disappear. There is today an extensive philosophy and even theology of play. However, there has also always existed a genuine piety that understands itself and its earthly existence as a game of God, as in the Protestant hymn: "In Him all things find their purpose and aim; Even what man achieves is God's great game."

he calls "an almost comic example of misunderstanding the basic nature of the dramatic in Hegel's *Aesthetik* (Bd. 1, 267)" [Otto Ludwig, *Shakespeare Studies*, trans. Ida H. Washington (Lewiston: Edwin Mellen Press, 2006), p. 137]. Hegel maintains, I believe justifiably, that in *Macbeth* Shakespeare, out of respect for King James, intentionally avoided mentioning the historical Macbeth's ancestral right to the throne in order to make him into a common criminal. In response to Hegel's reasonable argument, Ludwig hurries to comment: "Can one even conceive of the idea that Shakespeare depicted Macbeth as a criminal in order to please King James? I cannot." Under the spell of German aesthetics in 1850, when Ludwig was writing, perhaps it was not possible. Today we can very easily conceive of it. Ludwig is a perfect example of what I mentioned earlier about the German cultural tradition—its conception of the dramatic playwright and its preconceived notions of Shakespeare the dramatist.

25. Cf. Appendix Two. Concerning Wilamowitz-Moellendorf's definition of Attic tragedy, which is cited by Benjamin, cf. footnote 32 below. Concerning his quote from Wackernagel, cf. footnote 35 below.

With reference to the Kabbalists, Luther spoke of the game that God plays with the Leviathan for several hours a day. A Lutheran theologian even took Shakespeare's drama for a "Wittenbergian play" and made Hamlet into one of "god's players."[26] Both Catholic and Protestant theologians quote Luther's translation of a Solomonic passage: "when he put in position the bases of the earth: Then I was by his side, as a master workman: I was his delight from day to day, playing before him at all times; Playing in his earth."[27] In the Vulgate, the final phrase is: *ludens in orbe terrarum.*

This is not the place to explicate this obscure passage, nor to discuss the relation of church liturgy and its sacrifice to such a profound concept of play. In any case, Shakespeare's drama has nothing to do with church liturgy. It is neither religious, nor does it stand (like classical French theater) in a framework determined by the sovereignty of the state. The idea that God plays with us can elevate us to an optimistic theodicy just as well as it can lower us to a despairing irony or bottomless agnosticism. Let us thus leave it aside here.

In German the word "play" has numerous aspects and contrasting applications. Anyone who, following notes on a written or printed score, strokes a violin, blows a flute, or beats a drum

---

26. "In the end God puts all the dolls back in the box and begins the play anew with Fortinbras." Karl Kindt, *Der Spieler Gottes: Shakespeare's Hamlet als christliches Weltheater* (Berlin: Wichern-Verlag Herbert Renner KG, 1949), p. 95. Together with the other merits of this excellent book, Kindt is also to be praised for continuing the focus on the objective action of the play to be found in Karl Werder's Hegelian interpretation of *Hamlet*, thereby taking an important step in overcoming psychologizing interpretations. See Karl Werder, *Vorlesungen über Shakespeares Hamlet gehalten an der Universität in Berlin 1859-60* (Berlin: Hertz Verlag, 1875).

27. Proverbs 8:29-31, [*The Bible in Basic English* (Cambridge, UK: Cambridge University Press, 1965). The Luther translation reads: *Da er den Grund der Dinge legte, da war ich der Werkmeister bei ihm, und hatte meine Lust täglich und spielte vor ihm alle Zeit; und spielte auf seinem Erdboden.*]

calls everything he does in following the notes "playing." Whoever throws or hits a ball according to the rules of a game is also
"playing." Little children and frisky cats play with a special inten-
sity, delighting in the fact that they do *not* play according to fixed
rules but in perfect freedom. Thus all these possible and con-
tradictory meanings—from the dispensations of an omnipotent
and omniscient God to the activity of irrational creatures—can
be circumscribed by the concept of "play."

Even so we must insist that—at least for us poor humans—
there is in play a fundamental negation of the critical situation
(*Ernstfalles*).[28] The tragic ends where the play begins, even when
this play is tearful—a melancholy play for melancholy spectators and a deeply moving *Trauerspiel*. It is with Shakespeare's
*Trauerspiel*, whose "play" character also appears in the so-called
"tragedies," that we can least afford to ignore the unplayability
(*Unverspielbarkeit*) of the tragic.

## The Play within the Play: Hamlet or Hecuba

All the world's a stage, or so it had become in the already intensely
baroque atmosphere around 1600—a *Theatrum Mundi, The-*

---

28. See Rüdiger Altman, "Freiheit im Spiel," *Frankfurter Allgemeine Zei-
tung* 100 (April 30, 1955). The entire passage reads: "Play is the fundamental
negation of the critical situation (*Ernstfall*) and therein lies its existential
significance. One can only know what play is after experiencing a critical
situation. The fact that play is often fashioned after the critical situation does
not alter this fact." Using the concepts and terms formulated by Hans Freyer,
one could say that part of the essence of the tragic is that it cannot be incorporated into a secondary system, just as the secondary system has its own
rules that exclude the intrusions of tragic action, perceiving them only as disturbances, if it notices them at all. Hans Freyer, *Theorie des gegenwärtigen
Zeitalters* (Stuttgart: Deutsche Verlagsanstalt, 1955), p. 93. On the "state" as a
secondary system, cf. Appendix Two on Walter Benjamin and German Tragic
Drama. Perhaps some day a legislator, realizing the relation between freedom
and play or freedom and leisure time, will establish the simple legal definition:
play is everything that one undertakes in order to fill and structure legally-
sanctioned leisure time.

*atrum Naturae, Theatrum Europaeum, Theatrum Belli, Theatrum Fori*. Men of action in this epoch saw themselves on center stage before spectators and understood themselves and their activities in terms of the theatricality of their roles. This sense of the staged nature of the world existed in other times, but in the baroque epoch it was especially intense and widespread. Action in the public sphere was action on a stage and thus role-playing: "Nowhere are action and setting richer than in the life of those whose element is the court."[29] James I, as well, admonished his son to always remember that as king he would be on stage and all eyes would be focused on him. In Shakespeare's Elizabethan England the baroque theatricalization of life was still ungrounded and elementary—not yet incorporated into the strict framework of the sovereign state and its establishment of public peace, security, and order, as was the theater of Corneille and Racine in the France of Louis XIV. In comparison with this classical theater, Shakespeare's play in its comic as well as melancholic aspects was coarse and elementary, barbaric and not yet "political" in the sense of the state-centered politics of the time.[30] Yet as primal theater it was all the more intensely integrated into its current reality, a part of the present in a society that largely perceived its own actions as theater—a theater which consequently did not set up an opposition between the present of the play and the lived actuality of a contemporary present. Society too was on the stage. The play on stage could appear without artificiality as theater within theater, as a living play within the immediately present play of real life. The play on stage could magnify itself as play without detaching itself from the immediate reality of life. Even a double magnification was possible: the play within the play, whose possibility found its astonishing realization in Act

---

29. Caspar von Lohenstein's preface to *Sophonisbe*, quoted in Benjamin, [*The Origin of German Tragic Drama*, pp. 92-93].

30. See Appendix Two.

Three of *Hamlet*. Here one can speak even of a triple magnification, because the preceding pantomime, the "dumb show," once again mirrors the core of the tragic action.

The play within the play is something other than a look behind the scenes. Above all it must not be confused with the actor's play, which originated in the nineteenth century in the wake of social revolution. In the actor's play the scenery is torn down, the mask is removed on stage, and the actor presents himself in his naked humanity or as a member of an oppressed class. In the nineteenth century the elder Dumas made the famous Shakespearean actor, Edmund Kean, into the hero of a play; in our own century, Jean-Paul Sartre recently has done something similar with essentially the same effect. In both cases, a false public sphere is unmasked on center stage, i.e., in the public sphere of its own theater. Masks and scenery are cast aside, but only in the theater and only as theater. The spectators are educated about an individual psychological or social problem, and the play turns into discussion or propaganda. Modifying one of Karl Marx's angry outbursts, one can say here: the emancipation of the actors is achieved in such a way that they become the heroes, and the heroes become the actors.

In Shakespeare's *Hamlet* the play within the play in Act Three is not a look behind the scenes. One can speak, however, of such a behind-the-scenes view in Hamlet's meeting with the actors in Act Two. The conversation with them, their declamations, and the advice Hamlet gives them could become the point of departure for a genuine actor's play. But taken together these two acts are in fact the opposite. They do not serve the purposes of an actor's play but rather that of the pure play within the play. The actor who declaims the death of Priam weeps for Hecuba. Hamlet, however, does not weep for Hecuba. He is somewhat astonished to learn that there are people who, in the performance of their duties, weep over something that does not concern them in the least and has no impact upon their actual existence and situation. Hamlet uses this knowledge to sternly reproach himself, to focus upon his own situation, and to compel himself to action and the fulfillment of his vow of vengeance.[31]

It is inconceivable that Shakespeare intended no more than to make his Hamlet into a Hecuba, that we are meant to weep for Hamlet as the actor wept for the Trojan queen. We would, however, in point of fact weep for Hamlet as for Hecuba if we wished to divorce the reality of our present existence from the play on the stage. Our tears would then become the tears of actors. We would no longer have any purpose or cause and would have sacrificed both to the aesthetic enjoyment of the play. That would be bad, because it would prove that the gods in the theater are different from those in the forum and the pulpit.

The play within the play in Act Three of *Hamlet* is not only no look behind the scenes, but, on the contrary, it is the real play itself repeated *before* the curtains. This presupposes a realistic

---

31. Hamlet's Hecuba monologue (2.2.552-609) precisely defines his true task, his *cause* [in English in the original], and he reproaches himself severely for being "*unpregnant of his cause*" [in English in the original], or "der eigenen Sache fremd," as it is translated by Schlegel. But what is Hamlet's cause, his purpose? The question is all the more significant because in his Hecuba monologue Hamlet conceives the plan to capture the murderer through the play within the play—the plan of "The Mousetrap." Here, then, in this important question of Hamlet's cause as it unfolds in this soliloquy, we come across a curious discrepancy between the first edition of the play (the Quarto of 1603) and the later versions (the Second Quarto [1604-05] and the First Folio [1623]) more commonly used today. According to these later versions, Hamlet has only one cause: to revenge the king, who was rudely robbed of life and property. However, according to the first edition, which originated *before* James I's accession to the throne in 1603, the "losse" that Hamlet has suffered is a double one: "his father murdred *and a Crown bereft him*" (2.2.587; 1603 Quarto, p. 148), whereby the "bereft him" evidently refers to the fact that it is young Hamlet himself who was robbed of the crown. This second "motive and cue for passion" was a call to the irresolute James from the Essex-Southampton group *before* James's accession to the throne. *After* the accession to the throne, it had to be left out. For more on this topic, see Appendix One, Hamlet as Heir to the Throne.

core of the most intense contemporary significance and timeliness. Otherwise the doubling would simply make the play more
playful, more unlikely and artificial—more untrue as a play, until
finally it would become a "parody of itself." Only a strong core of
reality could stand up to the double exposure of the stage upon
the stage. It is possible to have a play within a play, but not a
tragedy within a tragedy. The play within the play in Act Three
of *Hamlet* is thus a consummate test of the hypothesis that a core
of historical actuality and historical presence—the murder of the
father of Hamlet-James and the marriage of his mother to the
murderer—has the power to intensify the play as play without
destroying the sense of the tragic.

It is then all the more crucial to recognize that this drama,
which never ceases to fascinate as a play, does not completely
exhaust itself as play. It contains components that do not belong
to the play and, in this sense, it is imperfect as play. There is no
closed unity of time, place, and action, no pure internal process
sufficient unto itself. It has two major openings through which
historical time breaks into the time of the play, and through
which this unpredictable current of ever-new interpretive possibilities, of ever-new, yet ultimately unsolvable, riddles flows into
the otherwise so genuine play. Both intrusions—the taboo surrounding the guilt of the queen and the distortion of the avenger
that leads to the Hamletization of the hero—are shadows, two
dark areas. They are in no sense mere historical-political connections, neither simple allusions nor true mirrorings, but rather
two given circumstances that are received and respected by the
play and around which the play timidly maneuvers. They disturb
the unintentional character of pure play and, in this respect, are a
*minus*. Nevertheless, they made it possible for the figure of Hamlet to become a true myth. In this respect they are a *plus*, because
they succeeded in elevating *Trauerspiel* to tragedy.

## The Irreconcilability of Tragedy and Free Invention

In relation to every other form, including *Trauerspiel*, genuine tragedy has a special and extraordinary quality, a kind of surplus value that no play, however perfect, can attain because a play, unless it misunderstands itself, does not even want to attain it. This surplus value lies in the objective reality of the tragic action itself, in the enigmatic concatenation and entanglement of indisputably real people in the unpredictable course of indisputably real events. This is the basis of the seriousness of tragic action, which, being impossible to fictionalize or relativize, is also impossible to play. All participants are conscious of an ineluctable reality that no human mind has conceived—a reality externally given, imposed and unavoidable. This unalterable reality is the mute rock upon which the play founders, sending the foam of genuine tragedy rushing to the surface.

This is the final and insurmountable limit of literary invention. A writer can and should invent a great deal, but he cannot invent the realistic core of a tragic action. We can weep for Hecuba. One can weep for many things. Many things are sad and melancholy. But tragedy originates only from a given circumstance that exists for all concerned—an incontrovertible reality for the author, the actors, and the audience. An invented fate is not fate at all. The most inspired creation is useless here. The core of tragic action, the source of tragic authenticity, is something so irrevocable that no mortal can invent it, no genius can produce it out of thin air. On the contrary: the more original the invention, the more rigorous the construction, the more perfectly the play works, then the more certain the destruction of the tragic itself. In tragedy, the common public sphere (which in every performance encompasses the author, the actors, and the audience) is not based on the accepted rules of language and play, but upon the living experience of a shared historical reality.

In spite of Nietzsche's famous formulation that the birth of tragedy arises out of the spirit of music, it is perfectly clear that music cannot be that which we designate here as the source of tragic action. In another and equally famous formulation, Wilamowitz-Moellendorff defines Attic tragedy as a piece of myth or heroic legend.[32] He insists that the origin of tragedy in myth must be consciously incorporated into the definition of tragedy; myth thus becomes the source of the tragic. Unfortunately, he does not remain consistent with this insight. In the course of his discussion, myth becomes the "content" in general and ultimately even the premise in the sense of a "story" (as one would say today) from which the writer "creates." That is once again a mere literary source. Nevertheless, the definition remains correct because it perceives myth as a part of heroic legend, which is not only a literary source for the writer but living knowledge shared by the writer and his public—a piece of historical reality to which all participants are bound by their historical existence. Attic tragedy is thus no self-contained play. An element of reality flows into the performance from the spectators' actual knowledge of the myth. Tragic figures like Orestes, Oedipus, and Hercules are not imaginary but actually exist as figures from a living myth that are introduced into the tragedy from an external present.

It is a different matter with Schiller's historical drama, where the question is whether or not the general knowledge of history that can be presumed of the audience establishes a collective present and a common public sphere. The answer to this question determines whether history becomes a source of tragic

32. Ulrich von Wilamowitz-Moellendorff, *Euripides Herakles*, Vol. 1, *Einleitung in die Attische Tragödie* (Berlin: Weidemann Verlag, 1889), p. 43 ff: "What is an Attic tragedy?" Wilamowitz-Moellendorff defines legend as "the sum of the living historical recollections of a people in a time when the people can only think concretely in the form of a history of a myth." According to Wilamowitz-Moellendorff: "An Attic tragedy is a self-contained piece of heroic legend, poetically adapted in the sublime style for presentation by a chorus of Attic citizens and two or three actors, and intended for performance as part of the public worship at the shrine of Dionysus." [Trans.: Cited from Benjamin, *The Origin of German Tragic Drama*, p. 106.]

action or only the literary source for a *Trauerspiel*. I do not think that knowledge of history can replace myth. Schiller's drama is *Trauerspiel*; it has not risen to the level of myth. As is well-known, he thought much about this question and developed his own philosophy of play. Art for him is a realm of autonomous representation. Only in play does one become human, does one transcend self-alienation and find true dignity. In such a philosophy, play must become superior to seriousness. Life is serious, and art is jovial; indeed, but the serious reality of the man of action is then ultimately only "miserable reality," and seriousness is always on the verge of becoming an animal brutality. The autonomous and higher realm of play can be opposed to both seriousness and life. In nineteenth-century Germany, the spectators of classical Schillerian drama saw world history as world theater and savored this drama as a form of self-edification, along the lines laid out in these verses from Schiller's *Homage of the Arts*: "When thou hast once the world's great drama seen,/ Thou comest back more rich to thine own soul."[33]

In Shakespeare's time the play was not yet a realm of human innocence and not yet divorced from the reality of human activity. Sixteenth-century England was far removed from the comfortable enjoyment of culture of nineteenth-century Germany. The play still belonged to life itself—that is, to a life full of spirit and grace, but not yet "civilized" (*poliziert*). It was a life at the first stage of an elemental departure from the land to the sea, the transition from a terrestrial to a maritime existence.[34] Such seafarers and adventurers as the Earl of Essex and Walter Raleigh

---

33. [Trans.: Charles T. Brooks, *Schiller's Homage of the Arts with Miscellaneous Pieces from Rückert, Freiligarth, and other German Poets* (Boston: James Munroe and Company, 1847), p. 15.]

34. [Trans.: Schmitt describes this shift in more detail in *The Nomos of the Earth*, pp. 172-84, and in *Land und Meer: eine weltgeschichtliche Betrachtung* (Stuttgart: Reclam, 1942).]

belonged to the elite. The play was still barbaric and elemental; it eschewed neither sensationalism nor buffoonery.

We have only mentioned with a word, as a counter-example, that high-philosophical theory of the play as an autonomous realm of true humanity. Shakespeare, with whom we are after all concerned, indeed utilized and incorporated historical and literary sources. But even in his historical dramas he had a different relation to history than Schiller did. We have already referred to Shakespeare's seemingly anti-historical arbitrariness. In his dramas based on English history, history is for him not even a literary source but simply a mouthpiece. His plays are always straightforward theater—burdened neither with philosophical nor aesthetic problems. As much as the avenger is problematized in *Hamlet*, this drama of revenge does not attempt a deproblematization through play, let alone a humanization through art or a birth of the human in the play. The author of this seamless drama feared neither allusions nor mirrorings, but he allowed genuine historical intrusions to stand as they are. Precisely in the figure of Hamlet, he encountered a concrete taboo and an existing contemporary figure that he respected as such. The son of a king and the murder of a father are for Shakespeare and his audience incontrovertibly existing realities from which one shrinks out of timidity, out of moral and political considerations, out of a sense of tact and natural respect. This accounts for the two historical intrusions into the otherwise closed circle of a straightforward play—the two doors through which the tragic element of an actual event enters into the world of the play and transforms the *Trauerspiel* into a tragedy, a historical reality into a myth.

The core of historical reality is not invented, cannot be invented, and must be respected as given. It enters into tragedy in two ways, and there are thus two sources of tragic action: one is the myth of classical tragedy, which mediates the tragic action; the other, as in *Hamlet*, is the immediately available historical reality that encompasses the playwright, the actors, and the audience. While ancient tragedy is simply faced with myth and creates the tragic action from it, in the case of *Hamlet* we encounter the rare (but typically modern) case of a playwright who establishes a myth from the reality that he immediately faces. But neither in antiquity nor in modern times could the playwright invent tragic action. Tragic action and invention are incompatible with one another and are mutually exclusive.[35]

Shakespeare's incomparable greatness lies in the fact that, moved by reserve and consideration, led by tact and respect, he was capable of extracting from the confusing richness of his contemporary political situation the form that could be intensified to the level of myth. His success in grasping the core of a tragedy and achieving myth was the reward for that reserve and respect that honored the taboo and transformed the figure of an avenger into a Hamlet. Thus, the myth of Hamlet was born. A *Trauerspiel* rose to the level of tragedy and was able to convey in this form the living reality of a mythical figure to future ages and generations.

35. Wilhelm Wackernagel, *Über die dramatische Poesie* (Basel: Schweighauser Verlag, 1838). Of course, for Wackernagel, the reality of tragedy is only the reality of *past* history; the reality of the present belongs to *comedy*. He is thus already on his way to historicism. But his erudition is still considerable. Hegel's influence on him is enduring and significant, broadening his horizon, and the wealth of penetrating judgments is astonishing. One example is his commentary on the figure of Don Carlos in Schiller's drama. He emphasizes its historical inaccuracy, in which "tragedy is displaced" by the deviation from historical reality. He also cites Jean Paul's statement concerning the reputation that attaches to great historical names and the myriad of situations that accompany the name. However, because he sees history not as present but only as past, it must ultimately become for him only a literary source. The same holds true for legend, similar to what we have already observed for Wilamowitz-Moellendorff. As a result, Wackernagel does not distinguish between *Trauerspiel* and tragedy, and he ignores the problem of the relation between play and tragedy. In this respect, Benjamin's references to Wackernagel must be refined. See Benjamin, [The Origin of German Tragic Drama, pp. 89 and 106].

# RESULTS

What are the results of our efforts concerning the problem of Hamlet?

1. The first is a rational insight that explains the unbelievable excess of existing interpretations of Hamlet. The riddle does not allow itself to be elucidated by the content of the stage play itself, nor by the inner relations of a self-contained process; yet, it also cannot be resolved through a recourse to the subjectivity of the poet because an objective historical reality penetrates into the play from the outside. The many interpretations pursued for over two hundred years are not rendered meaningless with this awareness, however. It is precisely through the inexhaustible abundance of ever-new interpretations and interpretive possibilities that the mythical quality of *Hamlet* is in fact confirmed. One might well say, however, that it would not make sense anymore to pursue interpretations that are carried out in a psychological style. The psychoanalytic interpretations of father and mother complexes were the last stage and, at the same time, the death spasm of the purely psychological phase of *Hamlet* interpretation.

2. We have distinguished mere allusions from true mirrorings of the contemporary historical present (Essex) and from genuine intrusions. If we recognize and respect in the taboo of the queen and the distortion of the avenger type the genuine intrusion of historical reality, we can allow both to exist for themselves and leave them open. The path then remains open

for a naïve approach to the play. One can then perform *Hamlet* as pure theater, as Jean-Louis Barrault did in 1952. The shadow of objective reality must nevertheless remain visible. Otherwise the play, namely the conclusion with the mixed-up rapiers and the poisoned wine and its many deaths, becomes a slightly crass, so-called tragedy of fate, and the play runs the risk of becoming a melodrama interlarded with clever reflections. In any case, even a naïve understanding of the play results in a better and inwardly freer representation than the continuation of attempts to deck out the two intrusions with philosophical or psychological superfluities.

3. As soon as we have found our way to a naïve understanding of the theater play, all historical and even anti-historical misunderstandings are overcome. We have already refuted one historical misunderstanding. It would be foolish to play Hamlet in the mask of James. This would be either a historical panopticon and nineteenth-century costume drama or, alternatively, the attempt to pump blood into a specter, a kind of vampirism. No archive, no museum, and no antique dealer with their kind of authenticity can conjure up the presence of a myth. Shakespeare's greatness resides precisely in the fact that, in the existing chaos of his time and the quickly antiquated flotsam of daily events and reportage, he recognized and respected the tragic core.

However, deliberate modernization as a reaction against historicism also misses its target, though it is understandable when one considers the grotesque misunderstandings of historicism and knows what egregious errors are associated with the word "history." Where history is only understood as the past and that which "has been," and no longer as present or real, the protest against period costumes becomes meaningful, and one must perform *Hamlet* in tails. But this is only a polemical reaction that remains bound to its enemy. Its result is no more than a momentary effect, and its consequence is a rapid self-destruction. From *Hamlet* in tails it is then hardly another step to Offenbachiana.

4. The final and greatest benefit, toward which the true ambition of my efforts concerning the Hamlet problem have been directed, can here at least be indicated in conclusion. It consists in the fact that in distinguishing *Trauerspiel* and tragedy, we can recognize that incontrovertible core of a singular historical reality that transcends every subjective invention and can then understand its elevation to myth.

As is generally known, the European spirit has demystified and demythologized itself since the Renaissance. Nonetheless, European literature has created three great symbolic figures: Don Quixote, Hamlet, and Faust. Of these, one at least, Hamlet, has already become a myth. All three are oddly enough readers of books and thus intellectuals, so to speak. All three are led astray as a result of the intellect. Let us pay attention, then, to their origins and provenance. Don Quixote is Spanish and purely Catholic; Faust is German and Protestant; Hamlet stands between them in the middle of the schism that has determined the fate of Europe.

This appears to me to be the final and greatest aspect of the Hamlet issue. We encounter in Ferdinand Freiligrath's poem, "Germany is Hamlet," and his allusion to Wittenberg an inkling of this connection. A horizon thereby opens up in which it makes sense to remind ourselves of a source of the deepest tragedy, the historical reality of Mary Stuart and her son James. Mary Stuart is still for us something other and more than Hecuba. Even the fate of the Atreidae does not affect us as deeply as that of the unhappy Stuarts. This royal line was shattered by the fate of the European religious schism. Out of its history grew the seed of the tragic myth of Hamlet.

# Appendix One:
## Hamlet as Heir to the Throne

For both the evaluation of Hamlet's behavior and character and the objective meaning of the dramatic events it is important to understand whether Hamlet was the rightful heir to his father's throne. If so, King Claudius would be a usurper with all the moral and legal consequences and ramifications of this concept. He would not only be the murderer of the father, but also would have directly violated the right of succession of the son. Hamlet would not only be the avenger of his father, but also the competitor for his own throne. The drama would not only be a revenge play but also a drama of succession.

It is, in fact, both, to differing degrees to be sure. In the first part, which extends to the middle of the third act, it is almost exclusively a revenge play and appears to have the call to revenge and its fulfilment as its sole content. In the second part, on the other hand, beginning with the successful exposure of the murderer, a struggle to the death for political survival is so predominant that the problem of the succession recedes and the audience hardly remembers it. Nevertheless, it is there. Indeed, one can even detect elements of a negotiation toward a compromise between King Claudius and Hamlet, a theme that runs through the play as a thin, barely noticeable strand and that first becomes visible when one connects together the points in act 1.2.108-9 (Claudius recognizes Hamlet as next in line for the throne and wishes to be a father to him), act 3.2.90-92 (Hamlet complains to the King that he is being placated with empty promises), and 3.2.342-4

(the succession in Denmark). The remaining acts of the play—
Two, Four, and Five—contain, so far as I can see, no hints of this
curious interposition of a compromise proposal that the murderer makes to the son of the murdered man.

John Dover Wilson devotes a careful analysis to the question of Hamlet's succession to the throne in *What Happens in
Hamlet*. His considerations pose the problem from the point of
view of the question: Was Denmark an elective monarchy? The
question is answered in the negative. Claudius is marked as a
usurper. Hamlet is presumed to be the heir and rightful successor to the throne in Shakespeare's drama. This appears to me to
be the proper conclusion. However, the connection with the contemporary situation of the years 1600-03 in England is here quite
astonishing. The question of the "Scottish Succession" that Lilian
Winstanley has placed at the center of her book on *Hamlet* cannot be suppressed, even with the best of efforts. Dover Wilson
demonstrates that for the succession in England an "election"
through a council took place that, for its part, respected the
announcement of the final will—the "dying voice"—of the predecessor. In this way, James had the "dying voice" of Elizabeth.
Hamlet gives his "dying voice" to Fortinbras, whereby he also
speaks of an "election" (5.2.354-55).

Both significant and insightful is Dover Wilson's remark that
one need not make a detour through the Danish constitution to
understand the legal situation of the succession in *Hamlet*: "For
if Shakespeare and his audience thought of the constitution of
Denmark in English terms, then *Hamlet was the rightful heir to
the throne and Claudius a usurper*."[36] Indeed, if the English public
thought of Shakespeare's *Hamlet* in English and not in archaic
Danish terms, as should be, in fact, historically obvious, then
Hamlet's connection with James and the Scottish succession is
palpable and cannot be suppressed.

---

36. Dover Wilson, *What Happens in* Hamlet, p. 30.

When Hamlet speaks of King Claudius as a thief who has stolen the crown from a "shelf" (3.4.100), then he appears to speak not only as the avenger of his father, but also as the legitimate heir to the throne. But insofar as the word "election" plays a role, Denmark appears as an elective monarchy. Today, elective monarchy is understood in opposition to hereditary monarchy. It is thereby generally assumed that the succession takes place immediately upon the death of the bequeather. The heir to the throne thus becomes king at the moment of the death of his predecessor, according to the formula: the dead bequeaths unto the living, *le mort saisit le vif.* In such a hereditary monarchy, Hamlet would already be King and Claudius a usurper. In an elective monarchy, the successor to the throne first becomes king through election. Hamlet has obviously not been elected king, while Claudius presumably has. He took measures to be lawfully crowned king immediately after the murder of his predecessor. It may be that he in this way used legal and legitimate procedures in order to steal the crown, but according to the form and the appearance, he was then the rightful king and not a usurper. Appearance matters a great deal in the law, and the law depends, as Rudolph Sohm says, essentially on form.

In light of this problematic situation, a legal-historical clarification is pertinent. Today, we distinguish sharply between elective and hereditary monarchies. By election, we mostly understand only a *free* election. Our current legal concepts have become positivist and decisionist. Our jurists are legalists, although in England less so than on the Continent. In order to comprehend the concepts of the "dying voice," the law of succession to the throne, and election, we thus need a legal-historical clarification that I would like to briefly attempt here.

Three different factors must be taken into account in the succession to the throne in the northern monarchies. The force and significance of each individual factor in relation to both of the others vary strongly according to era and nationality. Each individual factor remains, however, always recognizable as a particular independent force. Therefore, a word like *Wahl* or "election" must only be understood in the context of and in connection with the concrete order of an individual people and its ruling house.

The successor to the throne is, in the first place, named by the previous sovereign, his predecessor, as the expression of his final will. This is the "dying voice" with which Hamlet names Fortinbras, with which Elizabeth will name James and which, in the year 1658, the English attempt to attribute to Cromwell at his death in favor of his son Richard. This naming by the predecessor is an authentic designation and is in no way a non-binding proposition or a mere recommendation.

However, it is also no arbitrary selection over which the nominating predecessor could freely dispose. Normally, he is bound to name a member of his own royal clan, a son or brother or some other kinsman. The "dying voice" is, in other words, determined by the old blood right, which originally had a sacred character. Under the influence of the Roman Catholic Church, the sacred character was strongly relativized and repeatedly undermined. Its effects continued long after, however, and can still be recognized in James' writings on the doctrine of the divine right of kings. The divine right of kings is, in its historical origins, this sacred blood right.

In the history of our German kings, we have a famous exception that precisely as an exception validates the rule and the concrete meaning of a Germanic ordering of succession to the throne: the naming of the Saxon Duke Heinrich by the dying King Konrad, who was a Frank. Konrad did not name his brother, Eberhard, but rather the man of another clan as his successor to the throne. But he did this with a very remarkable rationale that strikes us as very poignant today: he ascertained to his dismay that fortune, *fortuna*, had abandoned his own clan of Franks, yet was clearly present in the clan of the Saxon Heinrich. This naming of the Saxon Heinrich by the Frankish Konrad, and the subsequent negotiations and events leading to Heinrich's accession to the throne (918-19), have been analyzed and described many times by important historians. The norm is thus confirmed in light of this exception; the predecessor names the successor to the throne according to the right of blood.

Alongside both of these factors—"dying voice," or naming, and blood right, or divine right of kings—an additional third factor arises: the acceptance of the successor designated according to blood right by important figures of the realm or a council that is composed of such figures or that is otherwise influential. In this case, there naturally occur various negotiations and decisions that could be characterized as *Wahl* or "election," even though they are something entirely different than that which one recognizes today as a free election, and even though the designated successor to the throne is something very different than an electoral candidate in the contemporary sense. Crowning, anointment, and homage then follow upon the acceptance of the designated successor by the election. There is also the acclamation of the attendant masses. In all these individual events by which the new appointment to the throne is carried out, one can detect something of "election." Yet it is inexact and misleading to speak immediately of an elective monarchy. All of these events together, from the designation by the predecessor to the ceremonial crowning, homage, and acclamation, constitute a unitary whole that can only be correctly understood within the context of its own time period and its own people.[37]

---

37. Fritz Rörig, *Geblütsrecht und freie Wahl in ihrer Auswirkung auf die deutsche Geschichte. Untersuchungen zur Geschichte der deutschen Königserhebung (911-1198). Abhandlungen der deutschen Akademie der Wissenschaften in Berlin, Jahrgang 1945/46* (Berlin: Akademie-Verlag, 1948); and E. Mayer, "Zu den germanischen Königswahlen," *Zeitschrift der Savigny-Stiftung, Germ. Abteilung* 23 (1902), p. 1 ff.

King Claudius, the murderer who prepared an abrupt and unforeseen death for Hamlet's father, robbed him not only of his life, then, but also of the possibility of naming his son Hamlet as the successor to the throne. He stifled the *dying voice* and violated young Hamlet's right of succession to the throne. It is thus not possible to characterize Hamlet as the legitimate successor to the throne and Claudius as a usurper simply in the way that John Dover Wilson does. Hamlet's direct, unequivocal right to succeed to the throne arises only from one single factor in the Nordic order of succession to the throne: the sacred blood right. In other words: from the divine right of kings that James always appealed to. Even from the point of view of the question: "was Hamlet the rightful heir to the throne?" it is impossible to disregard the contemporary connection between Hamlet and James.

In our footnote 31, we indicated the change in Hamlet's situation due to James' accession to the throne in the year 1603. In the version of the First Quarto that *predates* James' accession to the throne, both motives—revenge and his own right to the throne—are distinctly recognizable. In the following versions of the Second Quarto and the First Folio, the struggle over the succession to the throne becomes less important because it had lost its contemporary relevance as a result of James' accession to the throne.

# APPENDIX TWO:
## ON THE BARBARIC CHARACTER OF SHAKESPEAREAN DRAMA: A RESPONSE TO WALTER BENJAMIN'S *THE ORIGIN OF GERMAN TRAGIC DRAMA*

Shakespearean drama in general and *Hamlet* in particular is no longer religious in the medieval sense, but neither is it state-centered or political in the concrete sense that the state and politics acquired on the European continent through the development of state sovereignty during the sixteenth and seventeenth centuries. In spite of many contacts and ties with the continent, and some commonalities in the transition from the Renaissance and the Baroque, English drama cannot be defined by such labels. It belongs to the thoroughly peculiar historical evolution of the island of England, which had then begun its elemental appropriation of the sea. This great step provides us with the intellectual historical coordinates (*geistesgeschichtliche Verortung*) of Shakespearean drama.

Walter Benjamin distinguishes between *Trauerspiel* (tragic drama) and tragedy[38] and, in keeping with the title of his book, deals primarily with German baroque *Trauerspiel*. Nevertheless, the book is rich in important insights and perspectives both for aesthetics and intellectual history in general, as well as for Shakespearean drama and *Hamlet* in particular. Especially fruitful in my opinion is the characterization of Shakespeare in the

38. Benjamin, pp. 57-158.

section entitled "Allegory and *Trauerspiel*," which demonstrates that in Shakespeare the allegorical is as essential as the elemental: "Every elemental utterance of the creature [in Shakespeare] acquires significance from its allegorical existence, and everything allegorical acquires emphasis from the elemental aspect of the world of the senses."[39] In *Hamlet* this means that "the drama of fate flares up in the conclusion of this *Trauerspiel* as something that is contained, but of course overcome, in it."[40]

Benjamin's main point concerning *Hamlet* may be found at the end of the section on "*Trauerspiel* and Tragedy."[41] This point also refers to the conclusion of *Hamlet* (5.2). Benjamin believes that something of a specifically Christian sensibility can be discerned there because shortly before his death, Hamlet speaks of Christian providence "in whose bosom his mournful images are transformed into a blessed existence."[42] It is here that this age presumably succeeded "in conjuring up the human figure who corresponded to this dichotomy between the neo-antique and the medieval light in which the baroque saw the melancholic. But Germany was not the country which was able to do this. The figure is Hamlet."[43]

This is a brilliant passage in Benjamin's book. But then we read: "For the *Trauerspiel*, Hamlet alone is a spectator by the grace of God; but he cannot find satisfaction in what he sees enacted, only in his own fate."[44] I understand the antithesis between play and fate that is articulated here, but I must admit that this sentence—which directly precedes the reference to Christian providence—is otherwise obscure to me. I cannot suppose that

39. Ibid., p. 228.
40. Ibid., p. 137.
41. Ibid., pp. 157-58.
42. Ibid., p. 158.
43. Ibid., p. 157.
44. Ibid., p. 158.

in this passage Benjamin wanted to make Hamlet into a kind of "God's player" in a Lutheran sense, as the Lutheran theologian Karl Kindt has done.[45] Benjamin writes: "Only Shakespeare was capable of striking Christian sparks from the baroque rigidity of the melancholic, un-stoic as it is un-Christian, pseudo-antique as it is pseudo-pietistic."[46] In response, I would like to make the following remarks.

*Hamlet* is not Christian in any specific sense, and even the famous passage concerning providence and the fall of the sparrow (5.2.227-228) that Benjamin invokes does not alter this fact. Perhaps it escaped Benjamin's attention that Hamlet speaks of a "special providence," whereby we already enter into theological controversies about special and general providence. Furthermore, Shakespeare first names this kind of providence in the text of the Second Quarto [1604-05]. In the First Quarto [1603], the text reads: "predestinate providence," which already opens the infernal gates of theological strife and confessional civil war. In my view, it would have been more Christian to simply cite the passage from Matthew 10:29. However, the additional theologizing is consistent with the taste of the theologizing James.

Revenge is the actual theme in the first part of the play—until the murder of Polonius (3.4). At this point Hamlet stands between Catholicism and Protestantism, Rome and Wittenberg. Even his doubt about the ghost of his father that appears to him is determined by the antithesis between Catholic and Protestant demonologies that arose from differing dogmas of Purgatory and Hell. What can be called Christian here has passed through James, the son of Mary Stuart, who was completely caught up in confessional struggle. The only really Christian aspect of this first revenge part of the play is the prayer of the murderer in the soliloquy of 3.3.36-72. The second part of the play contains a

45. Kindt, *Der Spieler Gottes*—see footnote 26 (p. 39).
46. Benjamin, p. 158.

life and death struggle and the murder of the heir. As a motif, the murder of the heir belongs to the oldest of Christian themes (Matthew 21:38, Mark 12:1-12, Luke 20:9-19, Acts 7:52). No trace of this is to be found in Shakespeare's *Hamlet,* although Hamlet is unquestionably seen as the rightful heir to the throne.

Shakespeare's drama is no longer Christian. However, it also does not lie on the trajectory toward the sovereign state of the European continent, which had to remain religiously neutral because it emerged from the overcoming of confessional civil war. Even when this state recognized a state religion and a state church, it based this recognition on a sovereign political decision. Benjamin makes reference in his book to my definition of sovereignty.[47] In 1930, he expressed his gratitude to me in a personal letter. However, it appears to me that he underestimates the difference between insular England and continental Europe, and therewith also between English drama and the seventeenth century German baroque *Trauerspiel.* This difference is also essential for an interpretation of *Hamlet* because the crux of this play cannot be understood in terms of intellectual or aesthetic categories like the Renaissance and the Baroque. The difference can be characterized most quickly and accurately with a well-known antithesis whose richness of meaning is symptomatic for the intellectual history of the concept of the political. It is a question of the antithesis between the barbaric and the political.

Shakespeare's drama falls within the first stage of the English Revolution, if one grants—as is possible and reasonable—that it begins with the destruction of the Armada in 1588 and ends with the expulsion of the Stuarts in 1688. During these hundred years, the neutralization of religious civil war led to the development on the European continent of a new political order: the sovereign state, which Hobbes called an *imperium rationis* and Hegel described as a realm of objective reason beyond theology whose

47. Ibid., pp. 65-66, 74, and 239n.

main *ratio* put an end to the heroic age, the age of heroic law and heroic tragedy.[48] The century of civil war between Catholics and Protestants could only be overcome by deposing the theologians because they continually fueled this civil war with their doctrines of tyrannicide and just war. In place of the medieval order of feudal castes or estates arose a public order of peace and security created and maintained by the legitimizing achievement of a new entity: the *state*. Those thinkers who no longer looked to the church but to the state for deliverance from the hopelessness of the confessional civil war, among them the jurist Jean Bodin, were called politicians, *politiciens*, in a very specific sense in France, the foremost country on the European continent. The sovereign state and politics designate the antithesis to medieval forms and methods of religious and feudal domination.

In this situation, the word *political* acquires a polemical meaning and consequently the thoroughly concrete sense of an antithesis to the word *barbaric*. In the language of Hans Freyer,[49] a secondary system displaces elementary and primary orders that function poorly. The modern state transforms men-at-arms, the existing good order, alimentation, and lawfulness into organizations characteristic of the *state*: army, police, finance, and justice. Through these organizations, the state establishes what it calls public peace, security, and order and makes possible the situation of a "civilized existence" (*polizierten Daseins*). In this way, politics, police, and *politesse* become a remarkable troika of modern progress opposed to religious fanaticism and feudal anarchy—in short, to medieval barbarity.

Only in the presence of this sovereign state can the classical theater of Corneille and Racine emerge, with its classical, or more precisely, juridical, or—even more precisely—legalistic

---

48. G. W. F. Hegel, *Rechtsphilosophie*, paragraphs 98 and 218.

49. Hans Freyer, *Theorie des gegenwärtigen Zeitalters* (Stuttgart: Deutsche Verlagsanstalt, 1955).

unity of place, time, and action.[50] From the perspective of this sovereign state, it is understandable that Voltaire would see in Shakespeare a "drunken savage." In contrast, the German *Sturm und Drang* of the eighteenth century invoked Shakespeare in its struggle against French drama. This was possible because conditions in Germany at that time were to some extent still pre-state, if also no longer—thanks to the influence of state formation—as barbaric as in Tudor England. It was at that time that the young Goethe, under the influence of the Baltic Herder, delivered his fabulous speech, "Zum Schäkespears Tag" (1771), with its famous passage: "My dear Frenchmen, what do you want with Greek armor too large and heavy for you? That is also why all French *Trauerspiele* are parodies of themselves."

In many ways, Tudor England was on its way to becoming a state. The word *state* appears in Shakespeare and Marlowe with specific meanings that deserve a special etymological analysis.[51] However, it was precisely in this century from 1588 to 1688 that the island of England withdrew from the European continent and took the step from a terrestrial to a maritime existence. England became the center of an overseas empire and even the country of origin for the Industrial Revolution, without going through the constricted passage of continental statehood. She organized

50.  Lucien Goldmann states that Racine's theater and his concept of the tragic derived from the changing positions of Jansenism vis-à-vis Church and State. His book, *Le Dieu caché, étude sur la vision tragique dans les Pensées de Pascal et dans le théâtre de Racine* (Paris: Gallimard, 1955) only came to my attention after the page proofs of this study were already in hand. Perhaps there will be an opportunity to compare Goldmann's position and concepts with my interpretation of *Hamlet*.

51.  In my book, *Der Nomos der Erde*, I make reference to this fact in a larger context (pp. 116-17) [*The Nomos of the Earth*, pp. 143-45]. Such an etymology would of course require better information about questions of state theory and the history of the concept of the political than that provided in the otherwise fine book by Hans H. Glunz, *Shakespeares Staat* (Frankfurt am Main: Vittorio Klostermann Verlag, 1940). Important documentary evidence for a history of the word *state* can also be found in Bacon's essays.

neither a state army nor a police, neither a judicial nor a financial system in the sense of the continental state. Following the lead, first of seafarers and pirates, then of trading companies, England participated in the land appropriation of a New World and carried out the maritime appropriation of the world's oceans.

This is then the century of the English revolution (1588-1688), whose first phase saw the dramas of Shakespeare. One should not view this situation only from the past or present of that time—from the perspective of the Middle Ages, the Renaissance, and the Baroque. Measured in terms of the progress toward civilization that the ideal of continental statehood—realized, however, only in the eighteenth century—signifies, Shakespeare's England still appears to be barbaric, that is, in a pre-state condition. However, measured in terms of the progress toward civilization that the Industrial Revolution—only beginning in the eighteenth century—signifies, Elizabethan England appears to be involved in a phenomenal departure from a terrestrial to a maritime existence—a departure, which, in its outcome, the Industrial Revolution, caused a much deeper and more fundamental revolution than those on the European continent and which far exceeded the overcoming of the "barbaric Middle Ages" that the continental state achieved.

The Stuart dynasty was not fated to foresee any of this, and was thus unable to extricate itself from the religious and feudal Middle Ages. Therein lies the hopelessness of the intellectual and spiritual position that James occupied in his arguments for the divine right of kings. The Stuarts grasped neither the sovereign state of the European continent nor the transition to a maritime existence that England achieved during their reign. Thus they disappeared from the stage of world history as the great appropriation of the sea was decided and a new global order of land and sea found its documentary recognition in the Treaty of Utrecht (1713).

The ideas and formulations of this book were based on lectures that the author presented in the"Brücke" in Düsseldorf on 30 October 1955 at the invitation of the Volkshochschule der Landeshauptstadt Düsseldorf.

# AFTERWORD:
## HISTORICAL EVENT AND MYTHIC MEANING IN CARL SCHMITT'S *HAMLET OR HECUBA*

David Pan

### Carl Schmitt and Post-War German Literary Criticism

Carl Schmitt's 1956 book, *Hamlet or Hecuba: The Intrusion of the Time into the Play* is an oddity. How does this political and legal theorist, best known historically for his legal opinions and writings in support of the Nazis and linked theoretically to his ideas on sovereignty, decisionism, and the state of exception end up writing a book of literary criticism concerning Shakespeare's *Hamlet*? And why should we, either as readers of Shakespeare or of Schmitt, bother to consider this book today? The answer to both of these questions has to do with the specific way in which Schmitt's political theory, from the very beginning, presupposes a theory of representation that would explain the way that a legal and political order establishes itself in a specific time and place. In spite of his pronouncements against aesthetics and culture, a careful look at his political theory uncovers at its core an aesthetic theory that would ground political decisions and processes in the representations that create meaning in an immediate way for a particular public sphere. His work presents one of the most elaborate and complete attempts to imagine the link between aesthetics and politics, and his study of *Hamlet* demonstrates this link by establishing Shakespeare's tragedy as a defining myth for the developing English public sphere.

The ground-breaking character of Schmitt's theory is matched, however, by the potential danger of its effects. Defining the polemical meaning of his text at the outset, Schmitt characterizes his attempt to merge aesthetics and politics as a departure from the prevailing modes of literary criticism in the West Germany of the 1950s. Schmitt leaves out of his account, however, that the predominant "text-immanent" criticism was a reaction against the politicization of literature in the Nazi period by a *Germanistik* profession that had "devoted itself in 1933 to National Socialism with more enthusiasm than any other discipline."[1] So Schmitt's move to link aesthetics and politics could be interpreted as a hidden return to a National Socialist form of criticism. Indeed, Schmitt's rejection of a view of literature that isolates itself from reality is a reprisal of Heinz Kindermann's Nazi-era disdain for a literary criticism that holds that "[a]rt, and with it literature, should be assigned a space that remains beyond real life."[2] Kindermann's Nazi-inspired alternative is to link art to "life" and "reality" in such a way that "literature can only be understood, in its origins, its essence and its effects, out of the totality of this blood-filled, breathing life," a "life totality" that he immediately specifies as "racial" and "völkisch."[3] Schmitt's own

1. Klaus Vondung, *Völkisch-nationale und nationalsozialistische Literaturtheorie* (Munich: List Verlag 1973), p. 105. For accounts of Schmitt's own involvement with the Nazis, see Raphael Gross, *Carl Schmitt and the Jews: The "Jewish Question," the Holocaust, and German legal theory* (Madison: University of Wisconsin Press, 2007; Gopal Balakrishnan, *The Enemy: An Intellectual Portrait of Carl Schmitt* (London and New York: Verso, 2000); and Joseph Bendersky, *Carl Schmitt: Theorist for the Reich* (Princeton, NJ: Princeton University Press, 1983).

2. Heinz Kindermann, *Dichtung und Volkheit: Grundzüge einer neuen Literaturwissenschaft*, 2nd ed. (1937; Berlin: Junker und Dünnhaupt Verlag, 1939), p. 2.

3. Ibid.

similar attempt at linking art to politics could be considered, then, as a reactionary move to bring back the politicization of literary and aesthetic activity that characterized the Nazi period, and in fact his book's portrayal of the link between drama and politics emphasizes the ways in which political exigencies placed constraints on Shakespeare's artistic freedom.

But to simply paint Schmitt's argument with the Nazi brush ignores the fact that the critics such as Kindermann who so staunchly defended a Nazi form of criticism in the 1930s became the exact same critics who denied the relationship between literature and politics in the 1950s and with it their own complicity with Nazi ideology.[4] From this perspective, Schmitt's defense of the link between aesthetics and politics could be seen as a polemical pointing to the Nazi elephant in the 1950s literary lecture hall. If Schmitt's exile from German academia at the time put him in a unique position to unmask the hypocrisies of German literary criticism, his move also seems to be consistent with his steady contempt for those writers from the Nazi era who disavowed their previous work.[5] As the rejection of a link between literature and politics in the 1950s was in fact part of a very political attempt on the part of German literary critics with

4. On Kindermann's reinvention of himself, see Andreas Pilger, "Nationalsozialistische Steuerung und die 'Irritationen' der Literaturwissenschaft. Günther Müller und Heinz Kindermann als Kontrahenten am Münsterschen Germanistischen Seminar" in *Literaturwissenschaft und Nationalsozialismus*, ed. Holger Dainat and Lutz Danneberg (Niemeyer: Tübingen 2003), pp. 107-26. Other prominent examples of similar transformations include Benno von Wiese and Hans Schneider/Schwerte. On Benno von Wiese, see Klaus-Dieter Rossade, *"Dem Zeitgeist erlegen": Benno von Wiese und der Nationalsozialismus* (Heidelberg: Synchron, 2007). On Hans Schneider/Schwerte, see, for instance, Claus Leggewie, *Von Schneider zu Schwerte: das ungewöhnliche Leben eines Mannes, der aus der Geschichte lernen wollte* (Munich: Hanser, 1998).

5. See for instance the description of Schmitt's relationship to Ernst Jünger and Gottfried Benn after the war in Helmut Lethen, *Der Sound der Väter: Gottfried Benn und seine Zeit* (Berlin: Rowohlt, 2006), pp. 237-57.

a Nazi past to cover up their collaboration, Schmitt's continuing insistence on this link is at once a re-embracing of this past and a critique of the de-politicization of post-World War II literary discourse. Schmitt's intervention in German literary criticism is partly so difficult to evaluate because his critique of Nazis turned liberal, post-war critics coincides with an attempt to return to the anti-liberal impulses of both his own Weimar-era theories and his Nazi-influenced work.

Though it is tempting to dismiss him as one of the truly die-hard believers in the Nazi faith, his ideas and convictions need to be taken seriously precisely because of his intransigence in the face of both the catastrophe of Nazism and the disintegration of his own academic career. By arguing for the connection between aesthetics and politics, Schmitt set himself against real Nazis, but only by upholding convictions that these Nazis had in the mean-time repudiated, and it may be that Schmitt saw his intervention as an attempt to salvage a conservative legacy, against "really existing" Nazism and the "Conservative Revolution."[6] Schmitt's stance on *Hamlet* continues his anti-liberalism in a way that implicates liberalism, not only in a naïve denial of the political consequences of aesthetic structures, but also in the institu-tionalized cover-up of *Germanistik*'s Nazi past. To insist on the separation of art from politics is to argue that the Nazi movement was simply a political movement with no cultural underpin-nings. By contrast, when Schmitt argues, with the Nazis, that politics is a continuation of culture, the subtext is that the Nazi movement was part of a consistent unfolding of the trajectory of modern German culture, partly as institutionalized in its literary canon—within which Shakespeare played a key role—and the perspectives of academic literary criticism. Schmitt is implicitly raising the stakes here by considering the merging of aesthetics

6. On the differences between Schmitt and the writers of the "Conservative Revolution," see Joseph W. Bendersky, "Carl Schmitt and the Conservative Revolution," *Telos* 72 (Summer 1987): 27-42.

and politics to be more than just a Nazi phenomenon but part of the trajectory of any expression of political will. Seen in this way, Schmitt can consider himself to be continuing his Weimar- and Nazi-era critique of liberalism in a way that fulfills the traditionalist promise of his own brand of conservatism while at the same time rejecting the alibi of pure art mouthed by former Nazi collaborators refashioning themselves into liberals.

### Schmitt and Adorno

In spite of Schmitt's unrepentant conservative stance, his insistence on the connection between aesthetics and politics places his work in close proximity to another 1950s critic of the idea of pure art, Theodor Adorno. Though their political sensibilities are diametrically opposed and their main fields of study only overlap obliquely, their common stance against a post-war liberal consensus suggests that a comparison here is not only fruitful but perhaps necessary in order to understand the key issues at stake. In spite of their differences, both thinkers were committed to the idea of an enduring link between aesthetics and politics. Adorno's idea of aesthetic autonomy does not involve a total isolation of the work of art, but an understanding of how art always participates in a larger social process, even when it seems to be expressing something profoundly individual. In a radio address on the topic of lyric poetry and society, published one year after Schmitt's book on *Hamlet*, Adorno insists "that in every lyric poem the historical relationship of the subject to objectivity, of the individual to society, must have found its precipitate in the medium of a subjective spirit thrown back upon itself."[7] The historical violence that society imposes on the subject is reflected in the work of art as part of its structure. Though the "individual impulses and experiences" of the lyrical subject appear to be

7. Theodor W. Adorno, *Notes to Literature*, Vol. 1, ed. Rolf Tiedemann, trans. Shierry Weber Nicholsen (New York: Columbia University Press, 1991), p. 42.

pure invention, "they come to participate in something universal by virtue of the specificity they acquire in being given aesthetic form."[8] Through the aesthetic forming, the work of art acquires a social meaning, not through any overt allusions or influences, but through the inner unfolding of the work of art.

By giving primacy to this inner development, Adorno is able to recognize the intrusion of historical violence into the work of art yet also argue that this intrusion does not completely determine the aesthetic structure. Rather, historical violence can be read as the negative projection of the social situation out of the structure of the work of art, which still forms the historical material according to an aesthetic logic that can set itself up against the political determination. Consequently, Adorno links art to society by insisting that the element of particularity of the work of art will always lead back to something universal, and the status of this universal is ultimately the main issue:

> immersion in what has taken individual form elevates the lyric poem to the status of something universal by making manifest something not distorted, not grasped, not yet subsumed. It thereby anticipates, spiritually, a situation in which no false universality, that is, nothing profoundly particular, continues to fetter what is other than itself, the human.[9]

Adorno sets up two universalities against each other: the genuine universal of the undistorted and unsubsumed subject on the one hand and the "false universal" of the society that distorts subjects by imposing particular interests onto an otherwise unfettered humanity. Both find expression in the work of art. The false universality of society creates the pathos and isolation of the lyrical subject, and the genuine universality of a projected humanity creates the resistance to society that defines the autonomy of the work of art. By designating the false universality as the "particu-

---

8. Ibid., p. 38.
9. Ibid.

lar," Adorno defines it in terms of particular political interests as opposed to the freedom from violence in the genuine universality of a pure humanity. He is consequently able to show how works of art relate in their structure to a political realm that is the source of distortion and pathos in the work of art yet maintain an inner realm of purity from violence in the vision of reconciliation. The truth of the work of art lies in its resistance to the false universality of the world surrounding it. Adorno links art to politics by maintaining that the work of art preserves a space of genuine universality while at the same time registering in its structure the distortions that arise from the violence of particularist interests. The contradiction between these two moments creates the possibility for tragic conflict.

Schmitt focuses on the same opposition between the autonomous and the social in the work of art, but provides them with a different valuation. In his analysis he opposes the "play" character of a work of art, its status as literary invention, to its ability to integrate "an ineluctable reality that no human mind has conceived—a reality externally given, imposed and unavoidable. This unalterable reality is the mute rock upon which the play founders, sending the foam of genuine tragedy rushing to the surface" (45).[10] If Schmitt's opposition between play and reality matches up with Adorno's contrast between the genuine universality of the individual subject and the "false" universality of society, the two differ in their valuation of the two poles of the opposition. Schmitt refers to the political pressures and particular interests of a time period as precisely those forces whose direct influence on the work of art raise the play to the level of tragedy. What Adorno refers to as the false universality of particular interests is for Schmitt the "objective reality of the tragic action itself" (45), grounding art in reality and thereby granting art its seriousness.

---

10. References to page numbers in this edition of Schmitt's *Hamlet or Hecuba* will occur in parentheses throughout the text.

This difference in their evaluations hinges on their diverging attitude toward the existing socio-political order. From Adorno's perspective, Schmitt's grounding of the tragic in an externally given reality is simply a surrender to the false universality of society, a world of self-interest and instrumental rationality. By contrast, Adorno searches for a lyrical language that represents "language's intrinsic being as opposed to its service in the realm of ends" and treats the existing order as the source of the violence that distorts an otherwise unfettered subject.[11] But this critique of Schmitt that accuses him of acquiescence to an instrumental reality misses the point of his defense of the real as the ground of the tragic. Schmitt's invocation of "reality" does not reduce it to instrumentality but presumes an idea of reality that merges an ideal and a material aspect.

Significantly, Schmitt is just as critical as Adorno of a social order that reduces everything to instrumental rationality. In fact, Schmitt's 1923 *Roman Catholicism and Political Form* sets up a critique of bourgeois ideology that prefigures the *Dialectic of Enlightenment* in the way that it creates a dual critique of the bourgeois. If the Sirens episode of the Odyssey presents for Adorno and Max Horkheimer the vision of how "the enjoyment of art and manual work diverge as the primeval world is left behind,"[12] Schmitt insists similarly that bourgeois society "succumbed to the fateful dualism of the age," which is "expressed here, on the one side, by a rapturously overpowering music; on the other, by a mute practicality. It seeks to make 'true' art into something Romantic, excessively musical and irrational."[13] The irrational aestheticism of overpowering music is for Schmitt merely a romantic illusion,

11. Adorno, p. 53.

12. Max Horkheimer and Theodor W. Adorno, *Dialectic of Enlightenment: Philosophical Fragments*, ed. Gunzelin Schmid Noerr, trans. Edmund Jephcott (Stanford, CA: Stanford University Press, 2002), p. 27.

13. Carl Schmitt, *Roman Catholicism and Political Form*, trans. G. L. Ulmen (Westport, CT: Greenwood, 1996), pp. 20, 23.

while the materialism of mute practicality lacks a connection to ideals. For both Adorno and Schmitt, an autonomous art is merely the pendant to instrumental rationality.

They differ, however, in their assessments of how to resist this situation. When Adorno writes that "[t]he lyric spirit's idiosyncratic opposition to the superior power of material things is a form of reaction to the reification of the world, to the domination of human beings by commodities that has developed since the beginning of the modern area [sic],"[14] he assumes that a modern, secular order has done away with all ideal aspects and that the only refuge for true ideals is the work of art in its independent unfolding. But while Adorno still holds onto the idea of a substantive reason that would provide an objective basis for social order, Schmitt's analysis presumes that there can be no rational basis for ultimate values and that different value systems will always be in competition. The result is that ideals must be established politically, that is, they must displace alternative sets of ideals. Consequently, whereas Adorno tries to maintain, hidden in the work of art, the hope of a universal humanity, Schmitt takes the opposite tack of identifying the ideal aspect imbedded in every political form. Because he presumes a multicultural world, his defense of ideals takes the form of an attempt to link the material to the ideal in specific cultural forms, for example in the Roman Catholic Church. For him, the "formal character of Roman Catholicism is based on a strict realization of the principle of representation, the particularity of which is most evident in its antithesis to the economic-technical thinking dominant today."[15] In defending the representational aspect of the Catholic Church, Schmitt insists on those aspects of the modern world that continue to invoke substantive ideals against the threat of "economic-technical thinking." He locates this opposition to

14. Adorno, p. 40.
15. Schmitt, *Roman Catholicism and Political Form*, p. 8.

instrumental rationality in the political sphere because an existing political order cannot be a matter of pure instrumentality, but rather must always be grounded in a supporting set of values that is established against alternatives. So while Adorno sees the autonomy of art as the place where ideals have sought refuge in a modern age, Schmitt argues that such ideals are contained in political forms.

The political foundations of society are not an expression of particularist self-interest for Schmitt but rather a result of the fact that an ultimate ethical basis for society cannot be universally human but must always involve a particular theology that arises out of a specific tradition. In *The* Nomos *of the Earth*, Schmitt identifies land appropriation as the founding act of a culture, from which all else follows. Schmitt sees the overarching truth of culture, not in a vision of universal humanity, but rather in the historical event in which a particular guiding principle, a *nomos*, "becomes visible in the appropriation of land and in the founding of a city or a colony."[16] Though this may involve violence, Schmitt's interpretation of the word *nomos* emphasizes that it does not mean "law, regulation, norm, or any similar expression," but rather "the immediate form in which the political and social order of a people becomes spatially visible."[17] By emphasizing that every culture must be based on an overarching *nomos* that is specific to it, Schmitt lays out a theory of culture that is predicated on the assumption of a "structure-determining convergence of order and orientation."[18] This convergence of a political and social order with a particular tradition means that the establishment of a culture will involve both an element of violence by which the land is appropriated and an overarch-

16. Carl Schmitt, *The* Nomos *of the Earth in the International Law of the* Jus Publicum Europaeum, trans. G. L. Ulmen (New York: Telos Press Publishing, 2006), p. 70.

17. Ibid.

18. Ibid., p. 78.

ing metaphysical principle according to which life is organized within the appropriated space. If the two always converge, then every land appropriation occurs under the sign of a particular *nomos*, and by the same token every metaphysical ideal must have a specific manifestation. "*Nomos* is the *measure* by which the land in a particular order is divided and situated; it is also the form of political, social, and religious order determined by this process."[19] Every order is based on a particular orientation that defines the overarching principles according to which that order is organized. Consequently, ideals cannot exist independently of their real-world manifestation, and this manifestation in a particular time and place becomes defining for the ideals themselves. Schmitt's perspective provides a new way of looking at the ideal that links it much more firmly to the particular than Adorno's attempt to link the particular back to "language's intrinsic being."[20] Instead of insisting as Adorno does on "the idea of a free humankind" as the ultimate ideal,[21] Schmitt leaves the definition of ultimate ideals to the theological choices that a culture makes in its self-constitution.

For instance, though Schmitt argues that the *nomos* of a particular place is constituted by the fact of appropriating the land and then drawing lines that enclose this land and determine relations vis-à-vis neighboring spaces, he also points out that the Spanish and Portuguese conquest of America was predicated on the Catholic missionary task given to Spain and Portugal by the papacy,[22] indicating that this particular land appropriation was not an act without precedent, but rather was already imbedded within a theological framework. Later on, as the medieval order in Europe began to be replaced by interstate politics, both the

---

19. Ibid., p. 70.
20. Adorno, p. 53.
21. Ibid.
22. Schmitt, *The* Nomos *of the Earth*, p. 111.

idea of freedom and the civilizing mission of Europe became the basis for land appropriation and provided the outline for the *nomos* that governed both European interstate relations and the relations between European powers and the colonies.[23] This critique of liberalism as the ideology of colonialism poses a fundamental problem for Schmitt's theories. On the one hand, this unmasking of liberalism as a stand-in for colonialist appropriation feeds into Schmitt's long-running accusations against liberalism's pretentions to universality as simply an alibi for an underlying violence. On the other hand, the critique of liberalism in *The* Nomos *of the Earth* does not function as an argument against the legitimacy of its ideals, which seem for Schmitt to be grounded, not in any putative universality, but in the will of the people who adopt these ideals. So even if Schmitt criticizes liberalism's claim to universality, he is willing at times to accept liberalism as a legitimate particular ideology. As one ideology among others, it is another example of how land appropriation is never an issue of pure violence. Rather, it is always carried out on the basis of cultural ideals that legitimate conquest and colonization. Though violence and power relations participate in the process by which a *nomos* establishes itself for a society or for the earth as whole, the final form that this *nomos* takes will always result from a cultural mediation of these power relations.

This cultural mediation is not just ideology or propaganda for Schmitt, but affects the way in which political decisions are actually made to the extent that these decisions depend upon an orientation toward ideals when faced with a concrete situation. Though Leo Strauss has criticized Schmitt for defending the political itself as a "'state of nature' that underlies every culture,"[24] Schmitt's primary point in *The Concept of the Political* is that the

23. Ibid., pp. 209, 237.

24. Leo Strauss, "Notes on Carl Schmitt, *The Concept of the Political*," trans. J. Harvey Lomax, in Carl Schmitt, *The Concept of the Political*, trans. George Schwab (Chicago and London: University of Chicago Press, 2007), p. 105.

decision-making that leads to the friend-enemy distinction is a profoundly cultural one, having to do with fundamental values. His insistence on the cultural aspect of the political is a consequence of the fact that, as Strauss recognizes, Schmitt, in contrast to Thomas Hobbes's focus on the individual, clearly designates the state of war and thus the political as something that pertains to groups, to the point that the state can "demand from its own members the readiness to die."[25] Because the constitution of the group is a social process that depends on the establishment of a symbolic order, Schmitt's theory must conceive of the enemy, not as a threat to "bare life" itself, which would be the interest of the individual, but to a way of life, which is the primary interest of the group.[26]

> Only the actual participants can correctly recognize, understand, and judge the concrete situation and settle the extreme case of conflict. Each participant is in a position to judge whether the adversary intends to negate his opponent's way of life and therefore must be repulsed or fought in order to preserve one's own form of existence.[27]

Because what is at stake is not life itself, judgments about the enemy cannot be objective and rational calculations about how to save the most lives, but rather must be value judgments about the relationship between a potential opponent and "one's own form of existence." The appeal to the actual participants rather than to an outside observer as the only ones capable of making a judgment results from this cultural aspect of the friend-enemy

---

25. Carl Schmitt, *The Concept of the Political*, trans. George Schwab (Chicago: University of Chicago Press, 2007), p. 46. See also Strauss, p. 106; and Victoria Kahn, "Hamlet or Hecuba: Carl Schmitt's Decision," *Representations* 83 (Summer 2003), p. 75.

26. See David Pan, "Against Biopolitics: Walter Benjamin, Carl Schmitt, and Giorgio Agamben on Political Sovereignty and Symbolic Order," *The German Quarterly* 82.1 (Winter 2009): pp. 56-60.

27. Carl Schmitt, *The Concept of the Political*, p. 27.

distinction in which the final judgment depends on the concrete
situation and values of the judge rather than the application of
any rational principles. The enemy is not defined simply in terms
of pure violence or biological survival but in terms of the preser-
vation of a particular "way of life." Rather than simply defending
one's bare existence against the enemy, the decision establishes
a particular cultural form that must be defended against what
one judges to be alien and threatening to this form. The designation of the enemy is never simply "decisionist" in the sense of an
arbitrary act. Rather, the sovereign's decision is always bounded
by a cultural understanding of that which constitutes the group's
way of life and consequently that which would threaten this constitution.[28] Because the political determination of the enemy is
always based on a prior understanding of just what constitutes
one's own way of life, law and politics are inextricably tied to
a cultural context with a specific tradition that is susceptible to
influence by aesthetic mediations.

These examples of a kind of cultural forming of political
events do not, however, serve to completely affirm Adorno's idea
that the aesthetic resistance to domination can map out a world
of reconciliation free from violence. They do indicate, however,
possibilities for structuring and controlling violence through an
aesthetic reaction to a current situation and the imagination of
alternatives to it. Because the constitution of a socio-political
order involves a political realm in which a culture must establish
itself in the real world against alternative cultures, the process of
realization is not based primarily on instrumental means. The
ultimate measure that determines the entire order of a place does
not arise from the act of violence but from a naming. "A land-
appropriation is constituted only if the appropriator is able to give

---

28. See David Pan, "Carl Schmitt on Culture and Violence in the Political
Decision," *Telos* 142 (Spring 2008): pp. 49-72.

the land a name."[29] The focus on the name is important because the priority of the name insures that there is an element of "visibility, publicity, and ceremony" in the exercise of power that is opposed to the "satanic attempt to keep power invisible, anonymous, and secret." If secret power is linked to an instrumental and purely economic rationality that has more in common with "beehives" than humanity, then the name refers to the aesthetic aspect of power that is based on symbols and thus ideals that go beyond pure materiality. At the same time, Schmitt's insistence on the name is also part of his argument against the kind of universal humanity that Adorno invokes as the ultimate ideal imbedded in every work of art. Pointing out that "humanity and reason are not names," Schmitt argues that the use of such nameless principles provides a cover for the true holders of power. "Law is certainly power and appropriation, but as pure law it is only pure appropriation, as long as its authors remain anonymous, and the true sovereigns remain hidden in darkness."[30] If ideals such as law, reason, and humanity are posited as general and universal, they no longer refer to any specific set of principles and traditions but in fact become placeholders for the rule of a hidden sovereign. Schmitt's position, stated polemically, is that Adorno's appeal to a universal humanity could be interpreted as a similar strategy to that of former Nazi literary critics whose shift to a liberal defense of culture for its own sake masks the continuing hidden sovereignty of German national identity.

This means that the work of art for Schmitt, in order to attain a level of truth, must reflect this nomos, the foundational naming, and integrate it into its aesthetic structure. His example is Shakespeare's *Hamlet*, where he demonstrates how the name of the king, James I, determined the structure of the play. Schmitt shows in "The Taboo of the Queen" how the ambiguity of the

29. Schmitt, *The* Nomos *of the Earth*, p. 348.
30. Ibid., p. 349.

queen's guilt was dictated by a kind of political self-censorship in which Shakespeare was attempting to allude to Mary Stuart's guilt in the murder of her husband but could not make this allusion explicit because he needed to support James I's bid for the throne (pp. 16-18). Similarly, Schmitt argues in the following section that Hamlet's indecisiveness was a result of Shakespeare's depiction of James I's ambiguous position in the religious conflict between Protestants and Catholics (pp. 25-31). For Schmitt these historical intrusions into the play create a "surplus value" beyond the literary invention that "lies in the objective reality of the tragic action itself, in the enigmatic concatenation and entanglement of indisputably real people in the unpredictable course of indisputably real events" (p. 45). The givenness of a political situation as expressed in the name is consequently the unavoidable starting point for culture in Schmitt, and the work of art must integrate this situation in order to attain truth.

The implicit critique of Adorno's position is not that Adorno is too idealistic to recognize the hard realities of violence that rule the world. Rather, Schmitt's defense of the importance of the really existing socio-political situation understands this situation to be itself a merging of ideals with particularity. Schmitt takes every instance of a human "being in the world" to be grounded in the real-world establishment of an ideal. In this sense every land appropriation involves a merging of order and orientation, which is to say that every existing order contains its own set of ideals that mark it as the result of a specific tradition. The task of the work of art is not to invoke an undistorted subjectivity against such marking, but to take its measure, to trace in its structure the parameters and implications of the theological decisions that frame the socio-political order in that time and place. An interpretation of the work of art that claims to set itself beyond such particular value choices by referring to a universal humanity does not really do so, but rather tries to set up its own universalism as the basis of a new type of order that would exclude and demonize all previous cultures. From this perspective, Adorno's idea of a good universality based on humanity is not really universal at all, but tied to a specific culture and ideology that is, if anything, more exclusionary than other cultures. Adorno himself recognizes the culturally suspect character of the idea of universal humanity by noting on the one hand that "[i]n the name of humanity, of the universality of the human, German classicism had undertaken to release subjective impulses from the contingency that threatens them in a society where relationships between human beings are no longer direct but instead mediated solely by the market." But he must then confirm on the other hand that this goal reverted to a culturally limited one in which "classicism's concept of the human being withdrew into private, individual existence and its image; only there did humanness seem secure. Of necessity, the idea of humankind as something whole, something self-determining, was renounced by the bourgeoisie, in aesthetic form as in politics."[31] The problem here is not that Adorno identifies the universal element of the poem with a particular idea of humanity developed in German classicism, but that he takes this idea of humanity to be the source of a non-political and truly universal space in the work of art. Though he criticizes the historical development that failed to put such a universal humanity into practice, his project seeks to hold onto the objective utopian content of this idea.[32] From the point of view of a Schmittian critique of liberalism, however, Adorno's aesthetic theory ends up defending a particular political position that is organized around the ideal of humanity and thereby demonizes all other cultures that would defend their own particularity.

31. Adorno, p. 49.

32. For a more extended critique of Adorno's project along these lines, see James Gordon Finlayson, "Morality and Critical Theory: On the Normative Problem of Frankfurt School Social Criticism," *Telos* 146 (Spring 2009): pp. 7-41; and David Pan, "Adorno's Failed Aesthetics of Myth," *Telos* 115 (Spring 1999): pp. 7-35.

Moreover, Adorno sets up the liberal subject as the only one that might be undistorted and whole in contrast to all other subjects that are taken to be subjugated to the violence of particular interests. Schmitt's alternative is to imagine that every invocation of ideals involves the affirmation of a concrete order, a particular merging of order and orientation in which politics and aesthetics play equally determining roles. For him there is no undistorted subject, nor a totally free society. Rather, every subject comes out of a particular tradition that defines its commitments, and every social order establishes itself by means of an existential process within a theological context. The resulting aesthetic theory is inseparable from Schmitt's political theory, and the goal of both is to understand the process of political representation whereby a culture's ideals are translated into reality.

**Political Representation**

Discussions of Schmitt's ideas on political representation have often considered it to be merely a way of providing propaganda for maintaining the power of a strong executive who establishes a more or less dictatorial rule.[33] From this perspective, the typical schema used by literary critics for understanding Schmitt is to assume that politics determines the structures of the state on

---

33. See for example Jan-Werner Müller, *A Dangerous Mind: Carl Schmitt in Post-War European Thought* (New Haven, CT: Yale University Press, 2003); William Scheuermann, *Carl Schmitt: The End of Law* (Lanham, MD: Rowman & Littlefield, 1999); Renato Cristi, *Carl Schmitt and Authoritarian Liberalism* (Cardiff: University of Wales Press, 1998); John McCormick, *Carl Schmitt's Critique of Liberalism: Against Politics as Technology* (Cambridge, UK: Cambridge University Press, 1997; Stephen Holmes, *The Anatomy of Anti-Liberalism* (Cambridge, MA: Harvard University Press, 1993); Duncan Kelly, "Carl Schmitt's Theory of Representation," *Journal of the History of Ideas* 65:1 (January 2004): pp. 113-34; Jürgen Habermas, "The Horrors of Autonomy: Carl Schmitt in English," in *The New Conservatism: Cultural Criticism and the Historians' Debate*, ed. Shierry Weber Nicholsen (Cambridge, MA: MIT Press, 1992), pp. 128-139; and Richard Wolin, "Carl Schmitt, Political Existentialism, and the Total State," *Theory and Society* 19.4 (August 1990), pp. 389-416.

the one hand while representation provides the legitimation for these structures on the other hand.[34] In his attempt to rehabilitate Schmitt for democratic theory, Andreas Kalyvas has argued that, contrary to the prevailing view, Schmitt's project, especially in his *Constitutional Theory*, is to develop his theory of representation as the prerequisite for a genuinely democratic politics. Though Schmitt argues that there is no higher law for the decision than the decision itself, the success of the decision is not at all a given but depends upon both the activity of the sovereign authority and the acclamation of the people. The role of representation in Schmitt's political theory is to establish the link between sovereignty and the popular will.[35] To take seriously Schmitt's foray into literary criticism is part of an attempt to think through the legitimacy of a democratic form of politics in which political structures and authority are established through the mediation of a popular will rather than simply through the ideas of an intellectual elite. Because Schmitt sees the idea of a rationally based order as part of a liberal attempt to pass off a particular order as a universal one, his alternative is to consider representation as the mechanism and tradition as the space where an order attains a concrete form. In his analysis, each separate legal and political order derives from a specific cultural tradition, whose legitimacy lies in its ability to sum up and represent the popular will. His political theory is consequently incomplete without the explanation of how representation works, and *Hamlet or Hecuba* presents a key text in this explanation.

On a social level, Schmitt's approach avoids managerial solutions that would install a bureaucratic elite as the determiner of

34. See for example Kahn, p. 74; and Franco Moretti, *Signs Taken for Wonders: Essays in the Sociology of Literary Forms*, trans. Susan Fisher, David Forgacs and David Miller (London and New York: Verso, 1988), pp. 44-46.

35. Andreas Kalyvas, *Democracy and the Politics of the Extraordinary: Max Weber, Carl Schmitt, and Hannah Arendt* (Cambridge, UK: Cambridge University Press, 2008), pp. 146-62.

ultimate values. He imagines instead a democratic alternative in which a popular will establishes itself as the determiner of political structures. But the representation of the popular will is not simply a kind of referendum in which a simple majority establishes the rules. He recognizes in *Constitutional Theory* that a political unit must be founded on a set of basic principles that cannot be simply discarded through majority votes. Instead, such principles as are enshrined in a constitution must be established in a process that transcends the political opinions of the moment but at the same time represents a common political will.[36] Though his turn to the sovereign decision has been criticized as an attempt to short-circuit democratic decision-making, his recognition of the fundamentally metaphysical and therefore ungroundable quality of highest principles leads to an understanding of how the popular will underlies sovereign decisions.

Schmitt seeks to establish basic moral and metaphysical principles based on the formation of a popular will that arises out of a common striving toward spiritual ideals. He emphasizes in *Roman Catholicism and Political Form* that "all political forms and possibilities become nothing more than tools for the realization of an idea."[37] Because an idea lies at the foundation of every political order, Schmitt needs to explain how an idea establishes itself in reality as the lived reality of a people. The issue of representation is consequently the issue of the *link* between politics and the idea. This linking role of representation is crucial for Schmitt because it differentiates for him a merely aesthetic process from a representation in an emphatic sense. As Schmitt notes: "Representation is not a normative event, a process, and a procedure. It is, rather, something *existential*."[38] The existential

36. See Kalyvas, pp. 138-42.

37. Schmitt, *Roman Catholicism and Political Form*, p. 5.

38. Carl Schmitt, *Constitutional Theory*, trans. and ed. Jeffrey Seitzer (Durham and London: Duke University Press, 2008), p. 243.

character of the representation means for Schmitt that it is a final basis of existence, not just an aesthetic image or a form of entertainment. The representation exceeds a purely aesthetic play by having direct political consequences, and in this sense the representation coincides with the sovereign decision. By the same token, the decision does not establish itself through violence or pure power but through representation. The decision has a representational form, and representation has the significance of a decision.

Moreover, because the representation is "not a normative event," like the decision it cannot be derived from the idea, neither as a corollary to an established principle nor as a kind of propagandistic legitimation of such a principle. The idea is not the source of the representation. Rather, if the decision and the representation converge within Schmitt's decisionism, the establishment of the representational link functions as the founding moment. This merging of the representation with the sovereign decision makes the decision into the moment in which the idea itself comes into being through the establishment of the link to the concrete situation. The forging of the link is the crucial activity, and this activity consists of grounding the seeming concreteness of the notion of the existential in something that is "invisible": "To represent means to make an invisible being visible and present through a publicly present one. The dialectic of the concept is that the invisible is presupposed as absent and nevertheless is simultaneously made present."[39] Because the invisible is "presupposed as absent" and can only be made present in the representation, this representational process of making the invisible into something visible is for Schmitt the key action in establishing both a particular political form for a people and the presence of an idea. The aesthetic element here is not limited to the illusionary and playful but leads to an intensification beyond

39. Ibid.

normal reality. "Something dead, something inferior or valueless, something lowly cannot be represented. It lacks the enhanced type of being that is capable of an *existence*, of rising into the public being."[40] In linking the political to the idea, the representation transforms reality into an aspect of an idea while at the same time establishing the presence of the idea. This heightened state of being that is enabled by the representation becomes the basis for Schmitt's political theology, in which ideas are not prior but only come into "public being" in an aesthetic process that links political existence to the idea through the mediation of the representation. Because the representation must therefore speak to the people and at the same time awaken its highest principles and most noble character, the theory of representation is Schmitt's method of linking popular will to metaphysical ideals and also an indication of the aesthetic element in the process of political will formation.

Schmitt imagines that the representation is the source of order, and consequently the key aspect of sovereignty for Schmitt is neither violence nor reason, but authority. As opposed to Giorgio Agamben's approach, Schmitt tries to understand authority as part of a mechanism by which the political decision can gain credence within a reception sphere of reflective judgment. By understanding the decision as a judgment needing confirmation through the popular will, Schmitt is not limited, as Agamben is, to seeing authority as sovereign violence, the anomic opposite to the rule of law, and related immediately to bare life.[41] Instead, Schmitt sees authority as containing its own form of legitimacy based in a public reception of the decision. Yet, this public reception does not involve arguments and discourse either. While

40. Ibid.

41. Giorgio Agamben, *State of Exception*, trans. Kevin Attell (Chicago: University of Chicago Press, 2005), pp. 85-86. Victoria Kahn's critique of Schmitt is also based on the idea that "[f]or Schmitt, in contrast, sovereignty is not a category of legitimacy." Kahn, p. 70.

Kalyvas criticizes Schmitt for "excluding public deliberation and civic debate from the political expression of the constituent power,"[42] this objection ignores the circumstance that views about fundamental values that ground authority cannot be determined through rational debate. As value judgments, they can not be referred to any logical arguments. Just as Hannah Arendt defines authority "in contradistinction to both coercion by force and persuasion through arguments,"[43] Schmitt sees authority as an independent form of legitimation.

But as opposed to Arendt, Schmitt turns to aesthetic theory in order to understand authority, not as something bound up with a specific Greco-Roman or Christian tradition, but as a phenomenon that can manifest itself in different times and places, depending on representational processes. Because Arendt, taking over an idea from republican Rome, argues that authority is derived from the ancestors leading back to the foundation of Rome and that the fall of Rome signaled the end of this type of traditional authority, the only modern form of political authority she recognizes derives from the foundation of states by means of popular revolutions. As a consequence, though she tries to avoid this result, her notion of authority must in the end affirm violence as the final ground of authority as well. She attempts to differentiate a non-violent form of authority based on the ancient Roman use of a founding tradition from the past from a modern, Machiavellian invocation of political foundations as a violent action in the present.[44] But in fact in both the Roman world and the modern one, the founding of the state must include the violence of land appropriation in order to begin a tradition. The Roman avoidance of violence that she cites could only occur

42. Kalyvas, p. 124.

43. Hannah Arendt, "What is Authority?" in *Between Past and Future: Eight Exercises in Political Thought* (New York: Viking Press, 1968), p. 93.

44. Ibid., p. 139.

to the extent that their political order was already founded on a past violence and thus could dispense with a new violent foundation. Her pessimism regarding the ability of modern institutions to restore the lost efficacy of authority does not stem from the passing of the Roman model, but from her own conception that authority could only exist as a continuation of the Greco-Roman tradition. She is limited to this tradition, first, because it represents for her the only legitimate tradition that could ground authority non-violently and, second, because she has not investigated the representational mechanisms of authority that would explain how it could function in a variety of different traditions.

Schmitt takes an alternative route by interpreting authority as an aesthetic phenomenon based on the merging of order and orientation. Instead of being based on arguments or on pure violence, the development of a popular will adheres to structures familiar in the sphere of aesthetics, in which a particular producer creates an aesthetic experience that must be affirmed by recipients in order to have any value. The recipients of a work of art are not in a position to themselves produce the work of art, but they are the best judges of its validity. If, as Schmitt's arguments presume, a political judgment concerning values functions in the same way as Kantian "reflective" judgments on art,[45] then the reception of the political judgment is also crucial to its validity. As with aesthetic judgments, political judgments would not be able to ground themselves on any objective principles but can only be affirmed by their link to the judgments of others. This intangible link between the sovereign and the popular will is the main issue in the question of political authority. As Samuel Weber points out, the key issue in Schmitt's conception of the political decision is not just the pronouncement of the judgment "but rather what agency or office is *actually capable of imposing* such a decision

45. See William Rasch, *Sovereignty and Its Discontents: On the Primacy of Conflict and the Structure of the Political* (London: Birkbeck Law Press, 2004), p. 28.

*effectively.*[46] This ability to impose a decision effectively depends on the response of an audience, and the question of sovereignty is linked to the issue of authority as the mechanism for grounding the idea in the popular will.

But though the people's existence is the primal basis of all political order, the "people" as formless will is dependent upon an authority for its organization. Even if the political will of a people is the source of the life energy from which all political orders gain their power for Schmitt and this will therefore retains an immediacy absent from laws and procedures, it cannot create a form and organization for itself. It is constantly in need of mediation by an organizing authority, and the resulting interaction between popular will and sovereign authority forms the representational mechanism for the functioning of every political order, but especially in a democracy. "*Democratic legitimacy*, by contrast, rests on the idea that the state is the political unity of a *people*. The people are the subject of every definition of the state; the state is the political status of a people. The type and form of state existence is determined according to the principle of democratic legitimacy through the free will of the people."[47] Authority is not just an issue for monarchy or dictatorship but for democracy as well, and Schmitt's identification of a democratic legitimacy that also has a claim to authority shows that he has a more general theory of authority that does not just apply to the Roman tradition but that seeks to explain the functioning of authority in any form of government.

Because ultimate values and the establishment of authority cannot occur by force nor through persuasion by arguments, they must be based on "an ethos of belief" that is for Schmitt

---

46. Samuel Weber, *Targets of Opportunity: On the Militarization of Thinking* (New York: Fordham University Press, 2005), p. 35.

47. Schmitt, *Constitutional Theory*, p. 138.

the final ground of all authority and all politics.[48] In order to understand how this ethos of belief develops, Schmitt describes representation and identity as the two basic formative forces that determine the character of a political entity. Setting up the difference between them within a framework reminiscent of the Nietzschean opposition between the Apollonian and the Dionysian as two aesthetic forces,[49] Schmitt describes representation first as a forming force that, like the Apollonian, is defined by its ability to create an appearance in the world.

> Representation invests the representative person with a special dignity, because the representative of a noble value cannot be without value. Not only do the representative and the person represented require a value, so also does the third party whom they address.[50]

In distinguishing three types of representational form—aesthetic, juridical, and political—Schmitt highlights how all three must address an audience, and this "third party whom they address" acquires a value that is comparable to that of the representative. Schmitt here clearly uses the model of aesthetic reception as the specific case of a broader representational process that occurs, not just with works of art, but in juridical decisions and political will formation as well. Schmitt employs the German word "Repräsentation" in this context in order to emphasize the aesthetic aspect,[51] and when he notes that a state cannot exist without representation, it is not because a state must delegate responsibilities, but because it cannot exist only as a mechanism but must have a particular form that is established through an aesthetic representation of the political entity. "There is, there-

48. Schmitt, *Roman Catholicism and Political Form*, p. 17.

49. On the functioning of this opposition in Nietzsche, see David Pan, *Primitive Renaissance: Rethinking German Expressionism* (Lincoln, NE: University of Nebraska Press, 2001), pp. 40-62.

50. Schmitt, *Roman Catholicism and Political Form*, p. 20.

51. Weber, *Targets of Opportunity*, pp. 30-31.

fore, no state without representation because there is no state
without state form, and the *presentation* of the political unity is
an intrinsic part of the form."[52] Whereas in *Roman Catholicism
and Political Form* Schmitt is still just developing his notion of
representation and criticizes the possibility of the leviathan as a
state without representation,[53] this citation from *Constitutional
Theory* shows that he at this point rules out the possibility that
such a state could even exist. Representation understood in an
aesthetic sense but applied here to the state rather than to the
work of art becomes a necessary process in the formation of
political entities. This representational quality of political entities in turn explains the political significance of entities such as
the Catholic Church, which are not states but attain their political meaning based on their representational effects in society.
Politics for Schmitt is always based on an aesthetic representational dynamic.

Because aesthetic representation in politics is not just a case
of a manipulation of the masses, his idea of representation is not
an example of what Benjamin calls an aestheticization of politics.[54]
Nor do his aesthetics amount to a "mobilization through myth"
that serves "to preserve an ultimately static picture."[55] Schmitt
notes for instance that a legislature has an important representative aspect because the representation of the political unity of
the people is a public event and cannot be conducted privately.[56]
Significantly, he argues that the representative character of the
parliament is lost if the true decisions are made behind the scenes

52. Schmitt, *Constitutional Theory*, p. 241.

53. Schmitt, *Roman Catholicism and Political Form*, p. 20.

54. Walter Benjamin, "The Work of Art in the Age of Mechanical Reproduc-
tion," in *Illuminations*, ed. Hannah Arendt, trans. Harry Zohn (New York:
Schocken Books, 1968), p. 242.

55. Jan-Werner Müller, "Myth, Law and Order: Schmitt and Benjamin Read
*Reflections on Violence*," *History of European Ideas* 29 (2003): p. 466.

56. Schmitt, *Constitutional Theory*, p. 240.

and the functioning of the parliament becomes mere spectacle. The people must be convinced that the legislature has true deci- sion-making capacity in order for it to retain its representational function: "A parliament has representative character only so long as one believes that its actual activity lies in the public sphere."[57] At the same time, the work of art's "play" character becomes mere entertainment rather than representation if it is not linked to an element of reality. The link to reality transforms the mere play into tragedy.

These examples demonstrate that the role of the people in a democratic government as recipients of the representation is crucial. For in complementary opposition to the principle of representation, Schmitt isolates another tendency toward "identity" that is grounded in the people and that maintains a defining influence on the possibilities of representation just as for Nietzsche the Dionysian art force maintains a connection to a "primal unity" that grounds the Apollonian representation.[58]

> In the same way, there is no state without structural elements of the principle of identity. The principle of form of repre- sentation can never be instituted purely and absolutely by ignoring the people who are always somehow existing and present. That is impossible because there can be no repre- sentation without the public and no public without the people.[59]

The reception moment of representation requires there to be a public sphere and thus real people, who for Schmitt place a constraint on the possibilities of representation, even in an abso- lute monarchy. Significantly, however, the principle of "identity" merges with the reception moment of acclamation. The identity

57. Ibid., p. 242.

58. Friedrich Nietzsche, *The Birth of Tragedy and Other Writings*, ed. Ray- mond Geuss and Ronald Speirs, trans. Ronald Speirs (Cambridge, UK: Cambridge University Press, 1999), p. 30.

59. Schmitt, *Constitutional Theory*, p. 241.

of the people does not exist until there is a successful reception of the representation.

## Rhetoric vs. Aesthetics

Because Schmitt is concerned with linking politics to the idea, he is at pains to purge representation of any hint of an illusionary aesthetic, that is, an aesthetic that is isolated and does not form the link that he is seeking. His idea of representation is consequently based on "rhetoric," whose authoritative power he poses against "a rapturously overpowering music" on the one hand and "a mute practicality" on the other hand.[60] As opposed to these two bad alternatives, Schmitt argues that rhetoric is able to establish a link between the idea and a political reality by creating a public sphere in which three specific parties are addressed and acquire "a special dignity" and "a noble value": "the representative," "the person represented," and "the third party whom they address."[61] In the case of the Catholic Church, the Pope is the representative, Christ is the person represented, and the Catholic community is the addressee. Christ grounds the representation through a foundation in a concrete historical presence. The office of the Pope extends this initial historical event into the future through a chain of representatives, whose authority ultimately derives from the reality of Christ and whose political effect is to establish the Catholic community as a unity of values and political form.

Schmitt develops a notion of representation in which a particular figure derives authority, neither from a charismatic presence,[62] which would be an aesthetics detached from reality, nor a material power, which would be a kind of violence, but

60. Schmitt, *Roman Catholicism and Political Form*, p. 23.

61. Ibid., p. 20.

62. On Schmitt's opposition to a charismatic mode of leadership elaborated by Max Weber, see Kalyvas 158-159, and George Schwab, *The Challenge of the Exception: An Introduction to the Political Ideas of Carl Schmitt between 1921 and 1936* (New York: Greenwood Press, 1989), p. 71.

from an office with a historical tradition that mediates between values and reality. Schmitt emphasizes that the Pope is the only remaining representational figure in the modern age,[63] primarily because the Pope's authority is "independent of charisma" and "the priest upholds a position that appears to be completely apart from his concrete personality."[64] At the same time, the Pope's authority is also neither bureaucratic nor impersonal, "because his office is part of an unbroken chain linked with the personal mandate and concrete person of Christ."[65] The person of Christ grounds a historical tradition in which values and a "world-historical form of power" merge in the Pope.[66]

But as Kahn points out, for Schmitt the "paradigm of representation is incarnation,"[67] and it is the original historical presence of Christ that grounds the entire rhetorical chain. Because the foundational moment of representation is a historical presence rather than itself a representation, the basis of representation seems to lie in a materiality that is devoid of values, a form of violence, thereby opening up Schmitt's theory to the criticism that the idea of rhetoric is indeed merely an alibi for brute power rather than a genuine form of legitimation. Yet, his insistence on the historical event, evident in *Roman Catholicism and Political Form* and which Schmitt holds onto in aspects of *The Nomos of the Earth*, contrasts with the idea of a representational dimension of the founding decision that he moves toward in *The Concept of the Political* and especially in *Constitutional Theory*. In terms of the example of the Catholic Church, what is missing in Schmitt's theory of representation is an account of the representational foundations of Christ's world-historical significance that goes

63. Schmitt, *Roman Catholicism and Political Form*, p. 19.

64. Ibid., p. 14.

65. Ibid.

66. Ibid., p. 20.

67. Kahn, p. 73.

beyond the historical fact of his presence and explores the way in which his story was able to gain its original truth. In *Hamlet or Hecuba*, Schmitt makes an effort at such an explanation through his discussion of the way in which *Hamlet*, in transforming itself from *Trauerspiel* to tragedy, attains the status of myth. Though Schmitt puts together the building blocks of an essentially aesthetic theory of myth that would explain its functioning in both the ancient and the modern world, he continues to struggle with the ambiguity between a rhetorical explanation for the source of the tragic that would find its ultimate ground in an initial historical violence and an aesthetic explanation rooted in meaning and values.

When Schmitt transfers the rhetorical schema from *Roman Catholicism and Political Form* over to *Hamlet*, the representative is the figure of Hamlet, the person represented is James I, and the "the third party whom they address" is the Elizabethan audience. This particular audience is crucial for Schmitt, because he emphasizes that Shakespeare's drama is not based on the strict separation of art and reality upon which German drama would be premised after the 18th century but rather exists within a public sphere that bridges between the two realms through the presence of the audience, which "establishes a public sphere that encompasses the author, the director, the actors, and the audience itself and incorporates them all" (p. 35). As a result, Shakespeare's theater "did not set up an opposition between the present of the play and the lived actuality of a contemporary present" (p. 41). Schmitt argues here that, as opposed to the theater of "Corneille and Racine in the France of Louis XIV" or of "Lessing, Goethe, Schiller, Grillparzer, and Hebbel" in Germany (pp. 34, 41), Shakespearean theater was simply an extension of the representational forms that characterized political life outside of the theater, and Shakespeare's plays consequently did not function on a purely aesthetic level but on a rhetorical level as well.

The insistence on rhetoric is a call to recognize the political subtext of a literary stance. Rather than fleeing political questions by focusing on a purely aesthetic event, Schmitt argues for a rhetorical approach by interpreting Hamlet's reaction to the actor's play about Hecuba's weeping over the dead Priam as an example of a play that incites the audience to action. In this reading, the significance of the actor's play does not lie in its purely aesthetic effect but its rhetorical one of linking the play to action. Schmitt rejects the aesthetic enjoyment of the play because it does not make sense for people to weep over something that has "no impact upon their actual existence and situation" (pp. 42-43). But the bad example of such an aesthetic reception ultimately creates the proper rhetorical effect of the play, that is, the example of the weeping actor moves Hamlet to action. For Schmitt this scene models for the audience the proper rhetorical as opposed to aesthetic function of drama. In Schmitt's view, the proper role for Shakespeare's drama is not to create "aesthetic enjoyment" but rather a rhetorical effect in which the play's significance is not to be distinguished from the effect of political and religious representations outside of the theater (p. 43). The representation should be linked to a purpose and a cause and has the function of moving people to action. A purely aesthetic approach would be an abdication of this political role, and Schmitt seems to be implicitly chafing at how the liberal escape into aesthetics reaffirms the political subordination of West Germany to the hegemony of the United States.[68]

Against the retreat into aesthetics, Schmitt argues that the play within the play in Act Three of *Hamlet* can only avoid becoming untrue as play because it includes "a realistic core of the most intense contemporary significance and timeliness" (pp. 43-44). The main significance of the play within the play lies in

---

68. Schmitt discusses U.S. imperialism and liberalism as its supporting ideology in *The* Nomos *of the Earth*, pp. 281-308.

its ability to function rhetorically as part of the real historical conflicts that surrounded the original stagings of *Hamlet* in England. Specifically, Schmitt argues that, before James I's succession to the throne, the First Quarto version of the play of 1603 contained implicit support for James's bid, "a call to the irresolute James from the Essex-Southampton group before James's accession to the throne" (p. 43, note 31). The relevant line ("a crown bereft him") was removed in the later versions because James was already king. By functioning rhetorically to influence political events, the drama turns the success of the play into an implicit form of acclamation for the crowning of James I. This rhetorical purpose maintains a grounding of the drama in reality that is ultimately the basis for its tragic effect.

But while Schmitt provides convincing examples for how *Hamlet* functioned rhetorically within the context of the English political situation of the time, these examples also demonstrate a slippage between rhetorical and aesthetic effects in Schmitt's analysis. This ambiguity results from the fact that, while Schmitt refers to the Elizabethan-era audience as the proper public sphere for the rhetorical effects that he cites, he also invokes the subsequent 350-year reception of Hamlet as the relevant audience for determining the status of the play as a mythic tragedy. The splitting of the addressee into both the Elizabethan audience and the critical Shakespeare reception leads to a conflict between the rhetorical effect on the former and what must be referred to as an aesthetic effect on the latter, though it will be important to distinguish this understanding of aesthetic from the idea of purely aesthetic that Schmitt rejects. So while Schmitt provides an innovative analysis of the rhetorical meaning of the play as it was performed in Shakespeare's time, the rhetorical analysis ultimately proves to be incomplete as an explanation for the play's subsequent mythic status and its tragic effect.

The conflict between rhetorical and aesthetic effects becomes evident in Schmitt's examples of the intrusions of history into the play that ground its rhetorical function. He seeks to define how a historical circumstance comes to determine the structure of *Hamlet* by focusing on how Queen Gertrude's situation in the play mirrors that of Mary Stuart, who was suspected of having played a role in the death of her husband, Henry Lord Darnley, after she married his murderer, the Earl of Bothwell. Schmitt argues here that the refusal of the drama to make the queen clearly guilty or innocent of complicity with the elder Hamlet's murder was the result of a political situation in which Shakespeare could not make the queen guilty for fear of antagonizing Mary Stuart's son, James, but could not make the queen innocent out of consideration for a London audience that believed in Mary Stuart's guilt. In this historical intrusion into the structure of the play, Schmitt clearly identifies the political considerations that forced Shakespeare to create an ambiguity in the plot. As Johannes Türk points out,[69] the key to Schmitt's argument is that the political exigency forces the play to avoid the issue of the queen's guilt and thereby creates a lacuna in the structure of the play. The historical situation causes the otherwise pure play to become a serious tragedy to the extent that the play's structure must accommodate a piece of incontrovertible reality, not as a direct reference, but as an empty space. The structuring effect of an outside reality on an otherwise autonomous play transforms the play into tragedy by creating a link between the play and a political reality.

But the example of the taboo of the queen as the structural effect of the presence of Mary Stuart in the audience's consciousness remains inadequate as an explanation for the enduring significance of *Hamlet* to the extent that the audience for the mythic quality that Schmitt cites is not the same audience as the Elizabethan one that would have felt the need for the ambiguity concerning the queen's guilt. If the guarantors of *Hamlet*'s status

---

69. Johannes Türk, "The Intrusion: Carl Schmitt's Non-Mimetic Logic of Art," *Telos* 142 (Spring 2008): p. 78.

as mythic tragedy consist of the critical commentary and artistic re-creation within the long history of Shakespeare reception that Schmitt cites at the beginning of his analysis (p. 7), then the specific historical circumstances linking the taboo of the queen to the dispute over Mary Stuart would in fact be relatively insignificant for the tragic effect. The 18th, 19th, and 20th century audiences no longer recall nor feel concerned by the rhetorical context, and the mythic quality for subsequent generations that Schmitt wants to explain must in fact include some other mechanism. If Schmitt were to focus only on the issue of Mary Stuart's guilt as the source of the tragic effect, in spite of the lack of a meaningful rhetorical connection to non-Elizabethan audiences, he would have to fall back on the type of argumentation that he uses in *Roman Catholicism and Political Form*, namely that the initial specific personage establishes the beginning of a chain of representative figures that leads into the present. But because the tragic effect is ultimately based on an initial rhetorical effect that has lost its direct significance, Schmitt would have to treat the tragic effect as one that is primarily based in the auratic status of *Hamlet* as a generally recognized myth and not in the particular aesthetic effect that the play would have on a later audience. In this way, Schmitt would emphasize a founding historical event for explaining the mythic quality, but only at the cost of depriving the work of art itself of an aesthetic basis for its own authority. This authority would have to be based ultimately in an institutional support that enshrines *Hamlet* as part of a literary canon. But such an emphasis on the institutionalization of a literary canon would feed into the same kind of separation of the aesthetic sphere from reality that Schmitt set out to dismantle. In fact, he seems to have recognized this problem with the Catholic Church after writing *Roman Catholicism and Political Form*, leading him to move away from it as a basis of political form in the course of the 1920s and toward his more nationalist stance of the Nazi era.

Schmitt does not confine himself then in *Hamlet or Hecuba* to the line of argument in *Roman Catholicism and Political Form*, and he outlines another mode of linking play to reality in his second example of how the historical intrusion transforms a play into a tragedy, not just for Elizabethan England but for audiences that are centuries removed. This example explains the enduring significance by referring, not to a rhetorical effect, but to an aesthetic one whose content includes a consciousness of a historical situation. Affirming that the transformation of the figure of the avenger into "a doubtful, problematic hero" is the key to the play's tragic quality (p. 21), Schmitt argues that this transformation of the typical revenge drama was determined by an intrusion into the play of the historical figure of King James. Schmitt does not argue that the figure of Hamlet is supposed to directly refer to James but that this figure is determined by the indirect effect of the historical James, transforming the structure of the revenge drama so that the focus turns toward Hamlet's indecision: "the problematic of the figure of the avenger stems from the contemporary historical presence of Mary Stuart's son. The philosophizing and theologizing King James embodied namely the entire conflict of his age, a century of divided belief and religious civil war" (p. 25). It is at this point that Schmitt's argument leads to a historical context that includes but also goes beyond the specific situation of James and Mary Stuart, indicating a broader historical reality of religious conflict. By incarnating the religious schism between Catholics and Protestants, James's situation created the impulse toward indecision in the avenger figure, and this indecision is thus the consequence for the play of a breakdown of a world-historical representational form. "In times of religious schisms the world and world history lose their secure forms, and a human problematic becomes visible out of which no purely aesthetic consideration could create the hero of a revenge drama. Historical reality is stronger than every aesthetic, stronger also than the most ingenious subject" (p. 30).

Even though Schmitt explicitly rejects an aesthetic explanation for the play's significance, the details of his argument map out an aesthetic rather than a rhetorical effect. Hamlet's indecision in the play does not create a particular call to action but rather illuminates a human problematic. If the Reformation was a time in which Christianity as political form was undergoing an extreme crisis of representation, the play integrates the effects of this world-historical transformation into its structure. But if the play recapitulates in its structure a world-historical process, the effect is aesthetic to the extent that the recapitulation process does not encourage a specific action in the audience, but results in a new insight. Rather than promoting the play's direct participation in political representation, the play's link to history involves the ability of the play's inner development to create an awareness of the constraints built into a historical context.

Such a reading of the structural effects of a work of art on an audience leads Schmitt's argument much closer to Walter Benjamin's approach to the play in *The Origin of German Tragic Drama*, and several sections of Schmitt's book include implicit and explicit responses to Benjamin's ideas on tragedy and *Trauerspiel*. When Schmitt writes that "tragedy originates only from a given circumstance that exists for all concerned—an incontrovertible reality for the author, the actors, and the audience" (p. 45), he is insisting on the importance of historical context for determining the structure of a tragedy in the same way that Benjamin does in his own analysis of the spiritual effect that the Reformation had on both political life and dramatic form in the baroque period. Moreover, in his discussion of Hamlet's inaction, Schmitt accepts Benjamin's treatment of indecision as the primary characteristic of the baroque.[70] Yet, the two offer alternative interpretations for the nature of the historical context and

70. Samuel Weber's attempt to distinguish between Benjamin's focus on indecision and Schmitt's insistence on an "absolutely definitive and ultimate decision" fails to consider the arguments in *Hamlet or Hecuba*. Samuel Weber,

the way that this context determines the possibilities for drama. For Schmitt, the confessional struggles are the underlying historical reality that intrudes into the play in the person of James, who stood at the center of these conflicts. The source of the tragic is, however, still the concrete historical event that creates the "shadows" in the play that ground the tragic effect (p. 44). While Schmitt draws attention to specific events such as the murder of James's father, Mary Stuart's guilt, and the fate of the Stuart house, all tied to the confessional struggles of the age, Benjamin focuses on how the religious struggles transformed the relationship between worldly event and spiritual meaning. The key for Benjamin is that in the baroque period "religious aspirations did not lose their importance: it was just that this century denied them a religious fulfillment, demanding of them, or imposing upon them, a secular solution instead."[71] The religious schisms were central for Benjamin, not directly because of the religious conflict, but because these conflicts led to a hardening of positions in which the link between secular life and spiritual life was severed. Because religious structures had become stultified by the extreme polarizations, spiritual concerns could not be fulfilled directly through action in the world, and such action began to have a futile character. As a consequence, "the German *Trauerspiel* is taken up entirely with the hopelessness of the earthly condition. Such redemption as it knows resides in the depths of this destiny itself rather than in the fulfillment of a divine plan of salvation."[72] The baroque drama remains imprisoned within worldly events and actions at the same time as it is suffused with a melancholy sense of their spiritual meaningless.

"Taking Exception to Decision: Walter Benjamin and Carl Schmitt," *Diacritics* 22:3/4 (Autumn-Winter 1992): p. 18.

71. Walter Benjamin, *The Origin of German Tragic Drama*, trans. John Osborne (London: Verso, 1977), p. 79.

72. Ibid., p. 81.

Based on this separation between action and meaning, Benjamin offers an alternative understanding of the lacunae that make up the tragedy in which the key is not the concrete historical event but the structure of those events that excludes certain outcomes. The tragedy reproduces this structure and its exclusions in such a way that they become clear to the audience. In the case of *Hamlet*, Benjamin emphasizes that its greatness as a tragedy lies in the way that it was able to create a self-awareness of the spiritual emptiness of the world by reintegrating a spiritual perspective in a negative way, through the reflection on melancholy that is created by Hamlet's indecision. As opposed to the German *Trauerspiel*, which "was never able to awaken within itself the clear light of self-awareness," Benjamin affirms that "[i]t is only in [*Hamlet*] that melancholy self-absorption attains Christianity."[73] In his response to Benjamin, Schmitt rejects the idea that *Hamlet* is Christian in the medieval sense and insists that the play must be understood within a historical development in which England around 1600 was in a transition period from an earlier medieval period, in which religious issues were dominant, to a modern period characterized on the one hand by state-based institutions and on the other hand by the sea and the industrial revolution (p. 61). Yet, when Benjamin writes that "[o]nly Shakespeare was capable of striking Christian sparks from the baroque rigidity of the melancholic,"[74] he is referring precisely to this situation of a transition away from a medieval situation in which worldly events could be depicted as parts of a story of salvation. At the heart of the baroque for Benjamin lies a spiritual emptiness in worldly actions that can only be depicted as a lack. Shakespeare's achievement in *Hamlet* was to have allowed this situation to be made palpable as a lack, which could only be done if Christianity could be invoked as an absent

73. Ibid., p. 158.
74. Ibid.

desideratum. *Hamlet* is not Christian in the medieval sense but in the baroque sense of a spiritual dimension that still maintains its authority in a private sphere but has been cut off from a direct connection to worldly events.[75] The Christian aspect of *Hamlet* for Benjamin is not an explicit story of salvation but a spiritually grounded awareness of a melancholy imprisonment in a world of action that has been decoupled from salvation.

If Schmitt overlooks this key aspect of Benjamin's argument, it is because he is overly concerned with concrete historical events as the basis of tragedy and does not recognize Nietzsche's and Benjamin's focus on how the tragedy attains its effects through an aesthetic reception of historical problems. In spite of his critique of Nietzsche's aestheticism,[76] Benjamin approvingly cites his explanation for how an aesthetic structure can depict the lacunae of an age through the technique of musical dissonance.[77] Translated into tragedy, this dissonance creates a situation in which "[t]he structure of the scenes and the visual images reveal a deeper wisdom than the poet himself can put into words and concepts."[78] The analogy between the events of the play and the spiritual situation of the spectators who share a historical context creates the tragic effect through the structure of the drama's development, which leaves gaps. The lacunae exist first in a historical reality as possibilities foreclosed by the structure of events, and the tragedy recreates those lacunae in a way that makes visible what in reality is normally invisible because foreclosed as a possibility. The gaps of tragedy are not the result of political considerations that can be readily named but of a historical situation that forecloses certain events. The tragedy

75. Ibid., p. 138.

76. Ibid., p. 101-104.

77. Ibid., p. 108-109.

78. Nietzsche, p. 105; Benjamin, *The Origin of German Tragic Drama*, p. 108.

makes the absent possibilities visible through the development of the inner dynamic of the play.

Here, we can return to the discussion of Adorno and his approach to aesthetic autonomy as the basis for reflection on experience. Adorno conceives of the spontaneous character of aesthetic play as the source of insights that can disrupt and change the course of historical events. The play of art unfolds the historical reality through autonomy, not just as direct rhetorical effect. Though Schmitt is reluctant to affirm the importance of aesthetic play, his contribution is to note that the aesthetic insights of an audience do not serve merely to establish a utopian element but also provide the basis for the development of a political will. While this means that political form cannot develop without an aesthetic truth, the other consequence is that every aesthetic truth has concrete political implications.

If Benjamin and Adorno develop an effective theory of how aesthetic processes recapitulate a historical situation to an audience through their inner unfolding, Schmitt's theories are most useful in defining the political consequences of these aesthetic effects on an audience. Benjamin reveals the separation between spiritual ideal and worldly action as the source of the tragic effect in *Hamlet*, but his idea that the tragedy heralds the end of a demonic fate in which the hero is sacrificed but "his soul finds refuge in the word of a distant community" falls victim to the same kind of abstract universalism as we saw with Adorno if it is not linked to the establishment of a new myth and tradition.[79] In the case of *Hamlet*, the structure of the drama, while creating lacunae from the point of view of a Christian perspective, also establishes the representational foundations for a new of political theology of the nation-state. Here, Schmitt's insistence on the mythic status of Shakespeare's *Hamlet* indicates that the age of myth is still with us and that the modern era is to be dis-

79. Benjamin, *The Origin of German Tragic Drama*, p. 109.

tinguished only by the specific selection of myths and not by its overcoming of myth itself. But if *Hamlet* establishes a new myth, what is the political import of this aesthetic representation?

## Revenge or Regicide: Performing Politics as Play

Both Schmitt and Benjamin agree that the rise of *Hamlet* marks the beginning of the end of the confessional struggles. Schmitt argues that Hamlet's indecision reflected the undecidability of the religious civil wars, and Benjamin points out that these wars had disengaged spiritual questions from action in the world, thereby sundering the merging of real and ideal—order and orientation—that Schmitt affirms to be essential to the legitimacy and stability of political representation and, with it, social order. But this does not mean that order and orientation, world and values, must remain always separated in the modern world, nor does *Hamlet* reflect a "modern destruction of the traditional symbolic order" in order to become "one of the main myths of modernity as such," as Carlo Galli has argued.[80] To simply argue "that the historical 'task' effectively accomplished by [tragic] form was precisely the destruction of the fundamental paradigm of the dominant culture" would be to miss the structural role that tragedy played in the development of English culture in a direction that did not just delegitimize the absolute monarch but established the ground rules for a constitutional monarchy based on the identity of the English nation.[81] The achievement of *Hamlet* lay not only in its lacunae but also in its adumbration of a mechanism for political representation that reestablishes the links between order and orientation, merging aesthetics

80. Carlo Galli, "Prezentazione dell'Edizione Italiana" in Carl Schmitt, *Amleto o Ecuba: L'Irrompere del Tempo nel Gioco del Dramma*, trans. Simona Forti (Bologna: Società editrice il Mulino, 1983), pp. 22, 32. I would like to thank Amanda Minervini and Adam Sitze for allowing me to consult their unpublished translation of Galli's essay.

81. Moretti, p. 42.

and politics in a way that cements the relationship between the political self-awareness of a people and sovereign authority. If Hamlet's indecision indeed relates to the theological divisions of the age, the play does not end with an emptiness and a dearth of alternatives. It thematizes these divisions as a crisis of political representation in order to then sketch the outline of a new mode of representation that links popular will to sovereign authority.

The play begins with two forms of failed representation that correspond to the two empty terms that Benjamin indicates, a false rhetoric of power on the one hand and an impotent spiritual fervor on the other hand. The false rhetoric is connected to King Claudius and his attempts to establish his authority by means of spectacles such as the firing of the cannon to salute, at the beginning of the play, Hamlet's decision to stay in Denmark with the King and, at the end of the play, Hamlet's scores in the fencing match with Laertes (1.2.121-28, 5.2.246-58).[82] In both cases, when Claudius proclaims, "let the kettle to the trumpet speak,/ The trumpet to the cannoneer without,/ The cannons to the heavens, the heaven to earth,/ 'Now the King drinks to Hamlet'" (5.2.253-57), he creates a spectacle that is meant to link his voice to a heavenly affirmation of his love for Hamlet, a rhetorical attempt to obscure his true motivations. The pendant to this false rhetoric is the appearance of the Ghost, whose profound effect upon Hamlet is not based on spectacle so much as the "revelation" about the details of his father's death. As Jennifer R. Rust and Julia Reinhard Lupton argue, "the Ghost may signify an echo or guilty memory of a pre-Reformation theological order." But because this supernaturally revealed truth is private, secret, and without rhetorical or aesthetic effect, it remains, like the religious truths in the confessional conflicts had become, incapable of political representation, "the spectre of the ever-possible dis-

---

82. Citations from *Hamlet* in parentheses are to William Shakespeare, *Hamlet*, ed. Cyrus Hoy (New York: Norton, 1963).

solution of the sovereign."[83] To be sure, this is the event that first inspires in Hamlet the idea of vengeance, but, as an event purely within his imagination, it is cut off from any kind of representational authority. In fact, without any other confirmation, the Ghost remains merely an aspect of Hamlet's madness, as in his interview with the Queen when she fails to see the Ghost (3.4.133-42). If she had not herself had the misgivings about her marriage to Claudius that Hamlet points to, then the reappearance of the Ghost would only have served to reinforce her suspicions, and perhaps his own, about his madness (3.4.143-60).

As opposed to these examples of failed forms of representation—the empty spectacle of the illegitimate ruler and the fading political authority of religion—the plays within the play herald the mediating role of a form of representation that is neither pure spectacle nor private ghost but a public representation of audience experience. Although Hamlet's "Hecuba" speech seems to demand a shift from "played" feelings to real ones, both plays within the play become important, not because of a direct call to action but because of the self-examination to which each play leads in the audience that ultimately creates the link between private conviction and public authority. In the case of the actors' performance of Pyrrhus and Hecuba, the effect on Hamlet is to see analogies, first, between Pyrrhus and himself as avengers of a father's death and, second, between Hecuba and Gertrude as wives whose husbands are murdered. Both analogies serve to provide a model of behavior against which the real-life examples are measured and then found lacking. Hamlet has not yet avenged his father, and Queen Gertrude has married her husband's murderer. Though the performance of Pyrrhus and Hecuba presents characters that are far from Hamlet's own concerns, the key representational function of the play is to establish by analogy a link

83. Jennifer R. Rust and Julia Reinhard Lupton, "Introduction: Schmitt and Shakespeare," in this volume, pp. xxxiii.

to the situation of the specific audience, Hamlet, which allows a new insight. So when Hamlet exclaims, "What's Hecuba to him, or he to Hecuba,/ That he should weep for her?" (2.2.525-26), it is not to berate the actor or the play as being pure play but rather himself for his own failure of expression. As Kahn has pointed out,[84] the next lines do not emphasize the illusoriness of the play, as Schmitt suggests (p. 42), but indicate the intimate relationship between play and experience by pointing out that it is precisely the parabolic link between the two that would create the most effective representation. "What would he do/ Had he the motive and the cue for passion/ That I have? He would drown the stage with tears/ And cleave the general ear with horrid speech" (2.2.526-29). Hamlet is not denying the significance of the pure play but insisting on the contrary that an analogy between the play's structure and the personal experience of the audience (which is in this case himself) would create the most effective theatrical representation.

Hamlet's failure at this point is not simply a failure to act but in the first place a failure to arrive at a public expression of his personal situation: "Yet I,/ A dull and muddy-mettled rascal, peak/ Like John-a-dreams, unpregnant of my cause,/ And can say nothing" (2.2.533-36). The task here is not just for Hamlet to act, but to *speak*. The point is not the event of the act itself, but the way in which Hamlet represents himself so that his actions can attain a particular meaning. For the great danger that Hamlet faces is that his actions will be interpreted, not as revenge, but as regicide. In order to avoid this second interpretation, Hamlet's words cannot be simply his own, in which case Hamlet "Must like a whore unpack my heart with words/ And fall a-cursing like a very drab,/ A stallion!" (2.2.552-54). Instead of complaining in a way that emphasizes his personal situation, he must establish an interpretation of both Claudius's actions and his own to an out-

84. Kahn, pp. 85-86.

side audience in such a way that his actions, and not Claudius's, carry the support of a popular will. If Hamlet cannot establish a representational link between his inner motivations and those of a larger audience, his actions will be seen as arising "Out of my weakness and my melancholy" (2.2.568). Hamlet's actions can only attain the kind of transformative effect on the political situation of the court that he ultimately seeks if they have a representational significance that can establish a new form of authority. He insists then, "I'll have grounds/ More relative than this. The play's the thing/ Wherein I'll catch the conscience of the king" (2.2.570-72). If the point of the play is to give him a better justification for vengeance, Hamlet's move toward action in the form of the play is an attempt to bring himself out of his own subjective imagination and closer to a public representation.

This means, however, that effective action is not simply historical, as Schmitt argues, but must be theatrical. If Kahn is correct in pointing out that "Hamlet's metatheatrical reflections, along with his powerful aesthetic response to the players, help us see that it is theatrical or aesthetic form which allows for action that is not merely a repetition of the historically given," her simultaneous insistence on the "'aesthetic' autonomy of art" obscures the way in which the plays within the play are not autonomous but in fact merge aesthetics and politics.[85] Hamlet's staging of "The Mousetrap" is central for his revenge mission only if this mission is understood as a political rather than a private one. We can see this political aspect in the details of Hamlet's plan. In the first place, though Claudius has no concrete relationship to the characters in this play, the analogy between the argument of the play and his own situation leads Claudius to a self-examination whose emotional traces can be read in his gestures. The aesthetic aspect of the play creates an awareness in the audience of the meaning of its own actions. But in the second place, Hamlet's plan

85. Ibid., p. 86.

depends on the fact of an intimate relationship between aesthetic insight and political representation and therefore on the idea that the king's self-awareness cannot be hidden, but will necessarily affect the King's self-representation. This link between insight and representation guarantees that the play, as a public accusation of Claudius, can only damage his authority to the extent that he himself betrays the hidden meaning of his actions. At the same time, the play becomes an element of reality by revealing the conscience of the King, not just to himself nor just to Hamlet, but to an outside audience, beginning with Horatio, who must confirm Hamlet's own reading of Claudius's reactions (3.2.67-81, 3.2.266-70), and continuing on to "th' yet unknowing world" (5.2.364) to whom Horatio will speak at the end of the play and for whose sake he cannot be allowed to die but rather must be charged by Hamlet "To tell my story" (5.2.333). In beginning his revenge by staging the play, Hamlet imagines a world in which art leads to insight into the meaning of one's actions and this insight in turn becomes the basis of political representation.

The intrusion of reality into drama, then, does not come about in these plays through pure rhetoric but the creation of an analogy between the plot of the play and the situation of the audience that leads it to insight into the meaning of its existence and actions. The key in all of these representations is the public expression of such insight, and the main task of the play is to establish a means by which to cut through, first, the rhetoric of what seems, which is the mode of representation used by Claudius with his cannon fire and his pompous court as demonstrated in the encounter between Hamlet and Osric (5.2.81-177), and, second, the vagaries of personal beliefs and imagination in the case of Hamlet, who at the beginning of the play clings only to "that within that passes show" (1.2.85) as well as his private relationship to the Ghost of his father. While the performance of the story of Pyrrhus and Hecuba succeeds in bringing Hamlet out of his feigned madness and to a plan of action for confirming his suspicions, "The Mousetrap" puts the lie to Claudius's rhetorical support for Hamlet by revealing his true feelings to a larger audience. In both cases, the plays succeed only to the extent that they lead the audience to a particular understanding of the meaning of its existence. Consequently, Shakespeare's drama is an attempt to establish aesthetic insight over both rhetorical display and private conviction as the true basis of political legitimacy.

Hamlet's task after the plays within the play is to link an aesthetically established self-awareness to political representation. The final scene of *Hamlet* presents the proper form for vengeance that Hamlet seeks and has been waiting for throughout the drama, not a private affair while Claudius is praying, which would be "hire and salary, not revenge" (3.3.79), but a public event that reveals the inner convictions at stake and presents them openly for the judgment of the audience. It is only in the public duel with Laertes, attended by a public consisting of "*KING, QUEEN, [OSRIC] and all the STATE*" (5.2.203), that Hamlet himself can finally take the stage in a performance that merges theater and politics and have the opportunity to attain his vengeance in the only way that matters to him, in an act of political representation. During this performance, Hamlet only moves to enact his final vengeance once Laertes publicly declares "The king, the king's to blame" (5.2.305). But once this public declaration has been made, Hamlet stabs the King in the very next line, to the audience's refrain of "Treason! treason!" (5.2.5.2.308). The entire meaning and even possibility of Hamlet's killing of the King turns on the significance of these audience words, which Claudius still tries to interpret as support for his cause, responding, "O, yet defend me, friends. I am but hurt" (5.2.309). It is in this moment that the play is decided: when the assembled public, which has previously shifted allegiances from the old Hamlet to Claudius (2.2.343-47), then supported Laertes as a possible new king (4.5.97-106), now has the chance to intervene to help Claudius but fails to do so and allows Hamlet to finally kill him with the poison (5.2.310-11). The efficacy of the vengeance does not lie in the historical event, the action itself, but in the representational development of an audience judgment that can then be the foundation for the establishment of a political will in this audience. Hamlet understands this dynamic, which is why he must wait for the moment when his vengeance can take a public form and create a decision point in the audience, that is, when it can decide to withdraw its support from Claudius as legitimate ruler and transfer this support to Hamlet. Hamlet delays his transformation from melancholy madman to avenging prince until he can, in a moment of audience insight, transform the loyalties of the audience and establish a new legitimate rule, which is to be not only his rule, but the rule of a kind of sovereignty in which personal convictions and outward representation are aligned and presented for public acclamation. Hamlet's tragedy stems not from the lost legitimacy of Christian political representation nor from "a highly developed theoretical consciousness alongside a capacity for rash and violent thoughtlessness,"[86] but from the fact that he is unable to construct on his own the new audience for which he has been waiting.

Contrary to the idea that "[w]ith the modern tragedy, the principle of authority is dissolved,"[87] Hamlet establishes the outlines for a new concept of political authority that replaces a Christian framework with one that is based in the traditions of English language and history, including the history of its theaters, "for they are the abstract and brief chronicles of the time" (2.2.494-95). Because Schmitt recognizes that "the people appear only in the public, and they first produce the public generally,"[88] he can appreciate how the development of the English theater was coincident with that of the English nation, and he is there-

---

86. Rust and Lupton, p. xli.
87. Moretti, p. 56.
88. Schmitt, *Constitutional Theory*, p. 272.

fore willing to speak the name of this new national order in a way that Benjamin was not willing to do, preferring instead to invoke a future age of freedom in an ultimate overcoming of myth itself. Schmitt seems to forget his own pronouncements about the primacy of the political, however, when he refers to the new order as the one of maritime existence and the Industrial Revolution rather than insisting more emphatically on the proper name of England, as if a merely technical innovation could be more significant than a political-theological one (p. 67). But if Hamlet's attempt to link sovereign action with political representation founders on the missing unity of the Danes, his tragedy marks out the path toward the development of a successful English national identity. Though *Hamlet's* mythic significance is not based on the kind of intrusion of historical reality into the play that Schmitt describes in *Hamlet or Hecuba*, it does present the kind of merging of aesthetics and politics that Schmitt describes in his discussions of representation in *Roman Catholicism and Political Form*, *Constitutional Theory*, and in aspects of *The* Nomos *of the Earth*. As in *Constitutional Theory*, the pendant to representation in *Hamlet* is identity, which means that the self-awareness of the audience is the foundation for the reality of the representation, whereby this audience is at once the theater audience and the developing English public sphere. In this sense, aesthetics and politics are not merely linked but become two aspects of a single process of representation. If this reading brings Hamlet in proximity to Hitler in their common goal of merging individual action with political representation, it is because the origins of English national identity lead not only to the eventual consolidation of an English form of nation-state democracy but also to a British form of colonialism, just as the rise of the Nazis did not result simply from the German people's subjugation to Hitler but from their popular acclaim for his actions. In both cases political representation links popular sovereignty to modern forms of political violence, and this connection constitutes the overarching tragical history within which both Hamlet's and Schmitt's personal histories attain their own tragic meaning.

## ALSO FROM TELOS PRESS

Victor Zaslavsky
*Class Cleansing: The Massacre at Katyn*

Ernst Jünger
*On Pain*

Paul Piccone
*Confronting the Crisis: Writings of Paul Piccone*

Matthias Küntzel
*Jihad and Jew-Hatred: Islamism, Nazism, and the Roots of 9/11*

Carl Schmitt
*Theory of the Partisan*

Carl Schmitt
*The* Nomos *of the Earth
in the International Law of the* Jus Publicum Europaeum

Jean-Claude Paye
*Global War on Liberty*

Jean Baudrillard
*The Mirror of Production*

Jean Baudrillard
*For a Critique of the Political Economy of the Sign*

Gustav Landauer
*For Socialism*

Luciano Pellicani
*The Genesis of Capitalism and the Origins of Modernity*

Lucien Goldmann
*Essays on Method in the Sociology of Literature*